The Plan

Collected Short Stories & Poems
of
Mary Lelia Allen Smith
Written Between
1916 — 1957

Marjie Eckhout

Compiled and Introduced
by
Marjie Louise Smith Eckhout
1988

1st Edition 1995
Published by A.R.D. Service, Inc.

ISBN 0-9645968-0-6

To The Memory of Mary Lelia Allen Smith:

*This book is dedicated to
the children, grand children,
and great-grand children of
Lelia Smith,
from her daughters,
Barbara Jean
&
Marjie Louise*

The poems that you will find within
Have come, at random, from my pen.
Works of art they may not be
But they are all a part of me.
Tho' they may lack in metre and rime
My friends will read between the lines.
Forgiving errors as they have in me,
Will the meaning in them see.
Knowing the mood my heart was in
When each one fell from off my pen.

Mary Lelia Allen Smith

Introduction

Mary Lelia Allen Smith was born June 3, 1899 in Mecosta County, Michigan. Her parents migrated to Michigan, in a covered wagon in 1897 from Magoffin County, Kentucky. She was the first child born in Michigan; the ninth of a family of twelve.

She graduated on June 30, 1917 from Lakeview High School in Lakeview, Michigan as Valedictorian of her class. Her older sister, Lona, was the Salutatorian of the same class with only one-sixteenth of a point difference.

Lelia and Lona both received their Life-Certificate teaching certificates from Kalamazoo Normal College. On August 2, 1957, Lelia received her Bachelor of Arts degree from Western Michigan University, Kalamazoo, Michigan.

After graduating from Kalamazoo Normal College, she began her career at Gobles, Michigan, where she taught high school english. In 1920 – 1921, she served as principal and taught high school english at Grandville High School, Grandville, Michigan.

Miss Allen married and had two daughters, Marjie and Barbara. She taught in the Flint, Michigan school system for twenty years. From 1927 to 1944, she served in the English Department at Emerson Junior High School, Flint, Michigan. She was forced to resign because of illness.

Mrs. Smith and her husband Lee moved to Boyne Falls, Michigan in 1944. She regained her health and assumed teaching the sixth grade at Boyne City. She was with the Boyne City schools for eleven years. She was forced to retire a second time because of health reasons in the Spring of 1955. Mrs. Smith received many awards for her devoted services to the many boys and girls in Michigan.

Mrs. Smith died February 28, 1959 at Little Traverse Hospital in Petoskey, Michigan. She was buried at Boyne Valley Cemetary in Boyne Falls, Michigan.

Contents

Contents

The Arbutus

In secret cloistered woodlands,
For one who nature knows
In very early Springtime
The shy Arbutus grows.

Not so showy as her sisters
Lily white or haughty rose
But a sweetness uncompared
To her friends she does disclose.

Hard to find but lucky mortal
Her discoverer proves to be
For once found she does not wither
Buts stays sweet for you and me.

Sweetest flowers are never gathered
Where the common hordes do stray
Only in some sheltered woodland,
Do they greet the light of day.

To A Violet

In the very heart of the forest
In shady dale or brooklet bed,
Hiding in fear from the cruel world,
The sweet violet lifts her head.

Pure and shy and modest
And blue as the bluest skies
In her dewy innocence
She reminds us of baby's eyes.

Lucky is he who finding her
From her woodland baby eyes
A faith and love for Jesus
Feels in his heart to rise.

So search in the heart of the forest
Til you find this floweret blue
The message of her is faithfulness
And faithfulness will come to you.

March, 1917

Our Flag

Who does not thrill to that passing flag
As it floats in the breeze unfurled?
Emblem of our own dear country,
Foremost in all the world.
How carefully wrought in every part;
How we treasure every hue,
Those colors were well chosen,
The red, the white, the blue.
The red stripe stands for liberty,
For which we all would die,
We are pledged to preserve our country
And keep her colors floating high.
The white on our flag is holy,
T'will ever stand for peace
For fairness to all nations,
May strife and bloodshed cease.
But first of all comes liberty,
Our homes, our pride, our land,
If these things are in peril,
We can not idly stand.
As long as it's in our power,
Peace rules day and night,
But we won't give up our freedom,
Though for it we must fight.
The blue on the flag pleads loyalty,
A loyalty that will not fade.

Written April, 1917

Class Poem

'Twas the night before Commencement,
I was sitting alone in my room
Watching the town lights glimmering
In the June night's velvet gloom
The air was soft and balmy
And wafted on gentle wings
The sweet perfume of roses
That June coming always brings
'Twas a night to make one dreamy
And soon my thoughts did stray
To our happy days at High School
That were soon to pass away.
In those days we had made friends
And formed ties dear and true
That would gladden our lives forever
And make us remember you.
We have stored away in our memories,
In the recesses of heart and mind,
Treasures more precious than diamonds
And far more easy to find.
Your tokens of love and friendship.
Your smiles and words of old
We guard with a greater zeal
Than the miser guards his gold.
We will miss your happy faces
But our sorrow is made less
When we think that we'll be missed
By our friends at L.H.S.
The next year seniors will miss us

Class Poem (continued)

For the noble example we set them
Of perfect behavior and grace
In the strength of the wonderful friendship
That exists between us and them
We take this opportunity
Of offering advice to them
In order to be worthy of the place we leave
Dear Juniors, I beg of you
That you will be polite and dignified
And more earnest in what you do.
We know you dear Sophies are sorry
With your guardian angels to part
But we commend you to the care of you Juniors
And we hope in the kindness of your heart
That you will for our sake protect them
And this day start life anew
That you may set them as good an example
As we have set for you.
I see you Freshies are grieving
Your sorrow you cannot conceal
It gleams on your face and peeps from your eyes
How very forsake you feel
But we leave to console you, the Juniors
And we hope you'll appreciate
Their goodness and kindness and wisdom
And will love them for our sake.
Now to all of you dear schoolmates
We will bid a fond adieu
With the wish that life your pathway
Will with thornless roses strew.

June, 1917

9

Wanted . . . A Romeo

I have a charming balcony.
So perfect 'tis in truth,
That just a fleeting glance at it
Brings dreams of love and youth.

And when on balmy April nights,
The silvery moonlight from above
Gleams down upon my balcony
I linger there and dream of love.

I play then that I'm Juliet,
And in accents soft and low,
I slip out on my balcony,
And call my Romeo.

But listen hard as e'er I can
I hear naught in reply,
For my Romeo is but a dream
And ne'er answers to my cry.

I build dream houses all the time,
And I like to see them grow,
But somehow dreams don't satisfy
When I'm calling "Romeo".

I have a charming balcony,
And if the lights were low,
I think I could play as Juliet,
If . . . you would be my Romeo.

Written, October, 1921

The Plan

Oh life, oh death, oh mortal man
What is thy mission here?
In the great divine and wonderous plan
Thou man, frail, inconstant
Governed by possessions, love, hatred, fear
What is thy purpose? What thy destiny?
In **The Plan,** what part do you fulfill?

Man's Life is a puzzling thing, like the
Webs of countless spiders, interwoven, so is the
Life of man.
Crossed and recrossed by the threads of
Other lives, man pursues his course.
Then his goal is reached and all is o'er.

My web but started; a long road still ahead
I stop and glance behind.
The thread I have spun is one of a mesh
Crossed and recrossed with countless others.
Childhood friends, schoolmates, grand men
And women who left their influence on my
Young life, all these threads are interlaced
With mine.

Then I recall as I think of them, that
My line crossed theirs too.
What effect did it have on their web?
Did I inspire them to better spinning or did I
Help to undermine the work of many years?
Then all in a flash my mission came to me.
My work in the plan Divine.

The Plan (continued)

That work is this, — to so live that when my
Thread of life is crossed by fellow man
He shall be inspired to higher
Things and not entangle, himself
In my web and be drawn down
With me.
May the Onnipotent one who created
Mortal man help me to fulfill my
Mission.

Thoughts On Death

Somewhere down Life's Pathway,

Far off — or very near —

Stalks Death, a spectra grim.

Yet — of him I have no fear.

In life I've oft been foolish,

But I know that I've been brave.

If I could face this world unfaltering

Why should I fear the grave?

To know you'll have defeat

Before you ever start;

Yet to smile at those you meet

As you try to do your part

Takes courage. Those who that have done,

Though failing, — have yet their victory won.

Of Death they will not be afraid;

Rather go to meet him, undismayed;

Tired and weary of being brave

They may find solace in the grave.

Phantoms

Dead ghosts from out the past
Are haunting me today.
I cannot find a weapon
To frighten them away.
They all unite together
And firm against me stand.
In vain does duty threaten
And in vain does she command.
Though I try to drown my memories
In labors dull and grim,
They peep out from every corner,
And there's no forgetting them.
Think not a past is over
When you have barred the door.
It will return to haunt you
Forever ever more.
So make the present happy
To noble ghosts give birth
And you will gladly welcome them
Because you know their worth.

Fate

Is there a hand that guides us on
With a purpose clear in view,
Or do we wander here and there,
No plan to what we do?
My life is like a pattern
Of someone playing chess.
I don't always choose a move,
But I make it none the less.
I no more sit down and figure out,
With reason and with calm,
A clear, true course that I intend
To sail Life's ship upon,
Then in steps Fate. We'll call it that.
Any name would be as good;
And I am forced to do that thing
I'd vowed I never would.

Anticipation

If I could look ahead and see
The dull, drab monotony
That attends my usual day.
I would not rise so hopefully,
Nor prepare for it so blithefully.
But in bed I think I'd stay.
But knowing not what lies before
Nor what joy might be in store,
Each morn I open up my eyes,
And to myself I softly say.
"Something nice will happen today."
Then hopefully, I arise.
But I know that I am glad
That good days can't be told from bad
That my eyes can't penetrate
The soft green curtain that ever lies
Between them and the glad surprise.

Our Way

If our way seems hard and tiresome
And we don't like the bumps we get
Are we going to be a quitter
And stop to whine and fret?

Be thankful you weren't chosen
To set among the few
Whose path is strewn with roses
And pleasant tasks to do.

My Father

(September 8, 1862 – July 22, 1929. Born in Magoffin County, Kentucky. Migrated to Michigan in a covered wagon, with his family in 1897)

A tall, gaunt form whose age approached
To nearly three score years and ten.
A carriage proud, a fearless gaze,
That marked him among all men.
An Anglo–Saxon through and through,
But bred a mountaineer,
Fed on hardship and courage grim,
In a land devoid of fear.
O'er sixty years of grim life's blows
Have beat upon his frame;
But have not one atom bowed it
And his eyes remain the same.
Keen blue eyes, so frank and stern,
That once gazing into them,
One dreamed he had met Sir Galahad
Returned from battles grim.
Eyes, before which sin and shame
Would slink away and hide.
Eyes that taught me when a child,
That truth could not be denied.
A broad, keen mind that grew with age,
His advice became most dear,
And I leaned upon his counsel,
More and more from year to year.
Like a gnarled old oak by age unbent
That storms and hardships had endured,
Death struck him down without warning,
Of a disease that could not be cured.

My Father (continued)

And now all life seems empty,
A space that cannot be filled.
Those dear eyes are closed forever,
And my Father's voice is stilled.
I tell myself in my longing
That it still remains for me,
To try to be the woman
My Father would have me be.

Written July 30, 1929

To Ida On Her Fifty-fifth Birthday

On your birthday, Sister dear,
I write this poem for you.
May it bear my gratitude
To one that is kind and true.
Though fifty–five your age may be,
You're young in form and mind.
The Magic Fountain of your youth,
Is just that of being kind.
On many faces Age may paint
Disfiguring lines and wrinkles;
On yours there linger tender smiles,
And in your eyes are twinkles.
The eldest of a brood of twelve,
Born 'neath a Southern sky,
In being a mother to the rest,
Your chief duty was to lie.
Small time was yours for childish play;
You were old before your years.
Your own sorrows were put away
While you dried the others' tears.
Pleasures few have been your lot,
And much of sorrow and strife.
Perhaps that's why you so enjoy
The little things of life.
A tiny gift, a pleasant word,
Now mean so much to you.
A flower bright, a day in Spring.
Are to you ever new.

Ida (continued)

Though many tasks are near at hand,
You have ever time to spare
To do some deed of kindness
Or for the sick to care.
Of worldly goods you have but few,
Though you're rich in love and friends;
And being too kind and generous
Are the greatest of your sins.
The homeless and the helpless
Are welcomed at your door.
You're the friend of young and old,
And loved by rich and poor.
There must truly be a Heaven
Where folks like you can go,
And be in some way repaid
For the things they did below.
But we hope that you stay with us
A long time yet on earth;
And we will ever bless the day
That gave you, Sister, birth.

The Teachers' Bible

Job, Chapter 28

Surely there is money for the Governor and a tax which he can obtain more.

The Sales Tax was created for the schools, but lo, it came not to them. It became a General Fund and free is the distribution thereof.

Liquor was an ancient evil. Verily the people despised it. But our land was desolate and void of school. Crime stalked upon the face of the deep. With great sorrow and misgiving liquor was voted back. To run our schools said the martyrs.

Then we had a slogan "Drink beer and keep the schools open".

Man putteth forth his hand and drank often and deeply.

As for the schools, they closed. Where did the money go?

Where is the money for education? And where is the place of the teacher's salary?

The Board knoweth not the place thereof; neither is it to be found in the land of the living.

The Governor saith, "It is not with me", and the City saith, "It is not with me".

It cannot be taken from the Sales Tax. Neither can it be obtained from the sale of liquor.

No mention is made of the wherewithal of the teacher's existance.

How long, Lord, how long must we be underpaid by this indifferent generation?

The world saith that we should teach for the love of our work.

Verily we have done so. We have given no thought to the morrow and the morrow did not take care of itself.

The teacher hath no place to lay her head. May the Lord help her.

The P.T.A.

In the good old days, long years ago
When Johnny was a boy,
His parents dearly loved him,
He was their pride and joy.
So they washed his face and brushed his hair
And packed his dinner pail
And then they sent him off to school
Or maybe — 'twas his jail.
Behind the desk, a teacher stern,
An awe-inspiring sight,
Set him at work his R's to learn
And saw that he did it right.

She wasn't worried about his health,
Or about his height or weight,
She didn't know about his sight,
Or why he entered late.
For the school and home were far apart
"And never the twain could meet."
Though parents and teachers did their best
The Results were incomplete.
Johnny took home his examples
And father worked them out.
Why Johnny failed his Arithmetic
There was very little doubt.

He learned a lot of dates and facts
Though why he couldn't say.
Then went home to work the farm
And forgot them all straightway.

The P.T.A. (continued)

Then lo and behold: some teacher rare
Began this code to preach
"T'was not the subject matter
But the child we had to teach."
The school must teach him how to live
And first before they could,
They must understand the child
And what would do him good.

So in an earnest helpful manner
The teacher went to Johnny's home
Could they not work together,
Instead of struggling on alone.
Their purpose was one in common
To teach Johnny how to live
Would not a joint union
To the cause assistance give?
The parents were more than willing
The cause was one of worth,
In February o'er thirty years ago
They gave that union birth.

A small beginning it is true
But it spread from coast to coast
Soon a million earnest members
Was that great union's boast.
And now when children go to school
All up and down the land
They know that Parents and Teachers
For their good, Together stand.

From The Teacher's Point Of View

To have in our keeping throughout the day
The minds of the American youth
Is a privilege rare the world doth say
We believe it strongly, and come what may
We wouldn't dispute this wonderful truth
But for a moment I'm talking to you,
Talking — from the Teacher's point of view.

We return each morning with hopeful hearts
To our exalted place of work
With a high resolution to do our part
Determined never our duty to shirk
But a teacher's duty as it seems to you
Differs from a teacher's point of view.

We approach our desk with a high resolution
To uplift these children of men
To train their minds and inspire them on
So we inspect their teeth and nails again
And explain to them what soap will do
That is — from a teacher's point of view.

Excuses are read, we ponder long
To make our truancy complaint
We wonder if Johnie really did wrong
His own father's porch to paint
A simple matter it may be to you
But not — from a teacher's point of view.

We hasten thru the Home Room routine
And amidst the rush and turmoil
We toss a few truths as it were in a dream

From The Teacher's Point Of View (continued)

Praying they will fall on fertile soil
But knowing such cases will be few
We sigh — from a teacher's point of view.

It seems that the day has flown on wings
Though we have not been idle by far
As doctors and nurses and police men and things
And most of all their guiding star
A little teaching we have done, it is true
Very little — from a teacher's point of view.

A Teacher's Utopia but out of reach
In the land of far off dreams
Where a teacher would be allowed to teach
But that idea is passe' it seems
A teacher has something better to do
But not — from a teacher's point of view.

A land where teachers would be paid
According to their worth
Whether man or matron or maid
Where a pension could not have berth
Where your small checks would belong to you
Small — from a teacher's point of view.

A cynic, I know, I seem to you
But it is only a dream of mine
Small hope have I of it coming true
But such a Utopia would seem divine
Oh no — perhaps it wouldn't to you
But it would — from a teacher's point of view.

Citizenship

It matters not how much you know
In English, Science or Math.
Just carry home one little five
And watch your parents' wrath.

That little mark is very small
But it looms large in size
When it comes within the range,
Of our fond parents' eyes.

You see Dad knows the time spent here
Is for life a preparation.
On what we do with it depends
The success of our vocation.

Most parents know we can't get A's
In our classes every day.
It's grand to have a child so smart.
But we aren't built that way.

But they know that we can be
A sport at play or work.
And tho the task is often hard,
They believe we shouldn't shirk.

That is why when we've tried so hard
But just get a mark B–1
That Dad will clap us on the back
And say, "Fine, old chap, Well done."

Good honest folks who obey the laws
Are the need of the world today.
If you make a one in Citizenship
That's harder than making an A.

That one on your card will tell the world
Just how you're playing the game.
It will place you on the Honor Roll
Of those who respect their name.

Our Antiquated Youth

There is a little matter that's bothered me of late.

Why are our modern young folks so badly out of date?

They know the latest song hits, and wear the latest clothes,

But when it comes to travel, they're ancient, goodness knows.

They think that they can take a bike, in this traffic crowded day,

On a busy, modern pavement, and demand the right of way.

Or maybe it's a scooter, or a pair of roller skates,

They bring in on Transportation and try to crash her gates.

The lad who's from the country you knowingly call a seed,

But would he on the pavement, a donkey try to lead?

Of course you know he wouldn't. He's not that dumb by far.

He's parked his horse and buggy and drives a modern car.

And when he's out a stepping, how funny he must feel,

To see you simple youth on an antiquated wheel.

You laugh to see an ancient car on the pavement try to race.

Cannot you see that your old bike is much more out of place?

Your hard working, busy fathers have lots of things to do;

When you are bicycle bent for pleasure, must they turn out for you?

Every night the papers carry, to our ears a tale of woe;

Another death, another victim, of our youth who are so slow.

Transportation has kept marching. Have you given her no heed?

Better watch your skates and bikes, or you'll be called a seed.

The Great Invention Of The Time

The radio I've heard folks say,
Is a Miracle most rare
And all they talk about it seems
Is "what I got on the air".
They keep it on both day and night
So they won't miss one thing.
They can alternate between a fight
And a freak who cannot sing.
It's grand to get a Baseball game
Or the Stock Reports to hear,
And there's nothing like a Prize Fight
To be soothing to the ear.
The latest slang is heard each night
And little ones can listen in
On jokes that make us blush to hear
And parents sit and grin.
We criticize the movies
And censure them with care,
But let our children listen to
The filth that's on the air.
What program we will have tonight,
The family cannot agree
And I know whatever it is
It will make no hit with me.
The radio has its uses,
I'll admit it with a groan
But it's just another torture
In the great American Home.

Women Drivers

"Women drivers are no good
I never do them trust.
Will you please be careful
If drive a car, you must?"
These were the words you spoke,
And as you said thus and so
I angrily turned from your side
And to the car did go.
So you can not trust a woman
If she is going to drive?
Well, if it wasn't for a woman
Do you think you'd be alive?
Who cared for you when a baby
And taught you how to walk
Who guided your baby footsteps
And helped you learn to talk?
Who watched o'er you in the daytime
And protected you at night
And when you were ill, sat by you
Until the morning light?
Is it harder to steer a car
Then it is to sew a seam?
Is it harder to handle one
Than an electric sewing machine?
The hand that does the cooking
Or mixes up a cake
Might show a little caution
When the wheel she dares to take.

Women Drivers (continued)

Her patience has been proven
We know that she has nerve
For the greatest of life's missions
Tis her task the race to serve.
Did you ever know a woman
That did not courage show
And she's had experience in steering —
Men — where'er they go.
Your mother and your teacher
Do more to mold your life
Than any other factor
Unless — perhaps — your wife.
In the home or mill or factory
At the bedside of the sick
Where courage and skill are needed
And a hand that's sure and quick.
You will find a woman serving.
Doing her work the best she can.
Making the whole world better
And glorifying man.
The one that rocks his cradle
And is his guiding star
With a little help from man
Might learn to drive his car.

Dangers Of The Highway

Again has come the time of year
When folks are going places,
And in every heart there lies a wish
For the great wide open spaces.
We sit within a class room
Working hard on Math or themes,
When our eyes drift to the window
And our minds are lost in dreams.
Stretching straight and wide before us,
Lies a highway, broad and grand,
Leading on and ever onward
To an enchanted fairy land.
Forgotten now the dull math lesson
And our dreams develop wings,
Begins to plan a way to travel
Without car and other things.
But tarry, lad, wait but a moment
For that sober second thought.
Before you start upon that journey,
Do your really think you ought?
On that white enticing highway
Lurks a greater danger far,
Than giants and cruel villains,
Or the horrors of modern war.
All unseen there stalks a monster
Who each year his toll will claim,

Dangers Of The Highway (continued)

Of the boys who dare to hitch hike —
And Death is that monster's name.
You may think that you are careful,
And in road lore you are wise,
That you know when to wag your finger
And can pick them by their eyes,
But the figures are apalling
Of the ones who thought they knew,
And the jaws of death have claimed them.
Will you let him get you, too?
Don't you think it would be wiser
To bide awile at home
And wait for the family car, Sir,
Before you start to roam?

Once I Was Well And Light Hearted And Gay

Once I was well and light hearted and gay,
And busy as a bee the live long day,
But now I lie on my tummy the most of the time
With a hot water bottle across my spine
And count over the things I'll do no more.
And first and fo' most is waxing a floor.
Though the mattress I lie on, is a "Beauty Rest"
And the care I get is the very best,
I'm getting very tired of lying here,
And the last few days seem like a year.

Ode To Matrimony

Long years ago when I was young
I was told, and so were you
That "Marriages were made in Heaven".
I believed that it was true.
But being very observant,
I learned quite young in life
That usually a marriage license
Was a permit to abuse your wife.
The minister rang up the curtain
When he tied the sacred knot.
The play was full of action
And daily grew more hot.
You could tell a married couple
In any public place,
Where'er they went together,
By the boredom on their face.
I admired all young lovers
They were gallant and so kind.
They were tender to their ladyloves
And of all else seemed blind.
"That is true love", I would think,
"It's the kind that will not die".
"It will grow more kind and tender"
"Strengthen as the years go by".
But when they were once married,
I could scarce believe my sight,
They'd take up the old, old, cudgel
And begin their lifelong fight.
Of course, of happy marriages,
I think I've seen a few,
But they're always the exception
And then they scarce seem true.
True marriages are made in Heaven,
That saying should have read,
And the state of matrimony
I'm sure I'll always dread.

A Question

Little maidens sitting there,
Close to mother's knee
Face upturned, all intent
On what the story will be.
Two pairs of eyes, so frank and clear
And of the bluest hue
Like open windows in the sky
With heaven gleaming thru'.
Love and trust and faith shine there
But not one gleam of doubt
Sure that Mother — if not then God
Will keep all harm without.
Little Maidens, charming buds,
Eager to become mature
Longing for life and all it holds
To love, to work, to endure.

The story for a moment forgotten,
Pardon a mother's sigh.
I gaze into the future
Trying so hard to decry
Some token of mercy and kindness
For maidens such as these.
What chance have they of combating,
These innocents at my knees?

In a world of equality and freedom
Where woman has a mind of her own
In a few years, these two will stand
Facing it, mayhap, alone.
Should I then revise my teaching
And this very day begin

A Question (continued)

To reconstruct their vision
Of the world and maids and men?

If in this game of greed and gain
Those soft hands must compete
Will trust and faith bring aught to them
But the dregs of dire defeat?
Shall I begin today then
To help them understand
That this earth is a sordid place
The battle ground of man.
That the knights so pure and noble
They met in their story realm,
Have faded into the background
And a monster guides the helm.

That of sweet and charming maidens
There still exist a few
But their minds are quite befuddled
And they know not what to do.
Listening to their modern sisters
Who motherhood and homes discard
Who claim they must be modern
And to be modern they must be hard.
Temperance is old-fashioned
And Religion out of date.
Men go past the modest maid
And leave her to her fate.
Then shall I burn the fairy tales
And start this very night
To teach the truth unsugared
And start these maids a right?

Don't Cry, Little Girl

Don't cry, little girl, don't cry
Because your dollie can't walk.
I know you've tried over and over
To get her to laugh and talk.
If your doll were a real, real baby
Like others you may know
She would laugh and coo awhile dear,
But you could not keep her so.
Soon she would grow bigger
And then you would have to part.
Or maybe she would grow heedless
And then could break your heart.
So don't cry for a real baby, dear,
Your own is much better for you.
She will never, never leave you
And her heart will ever be true.

Don't cry, little girl, don't cry,
If your love has feet of clay
If the hopes and plans you had
Are but dreams of yesterday.
You decked him out in splendor
With all virtues true and fine
You exalted him above a mortal
And thought of him as divine.
Mayhap he's of grosser metal
Than you had thought him to be
But a love like you've found together
Is a thing of purity.

To Barbara On Her Passing Out Of The Elementary School

You have passed the Sixth Grade, Barbara;
Why, it seems scarce yesterday when
I made such great preparations
For your school life to begin.
I can still see your little blue dress,
And how you had longed for the day:
The day I had dreaded and hated
For it would steal my baby away.
You seemed so little and helpless,
You see, you were scarcely five,
And I had a silly notion
That I might not see you again alive.
How I hated my job that morning
Because it took me away from you.
I wanted to take you to school that day
As other girls' mothers would do.
I cherish the memory, dear Barbara,
That through these busy years,
You have always told your mother
Your hopes and childish fears.
I have missed your little programs
And other things too, I guess,
But with a more trusting, confiding daughter
No mother was ever blest.
And I'll try never to fail you, Barbara,
When you come to me for advice.
If for myself I have been ignorant,
For you I must ever be wise.
The next lap on your journey,
Those years in Junior High,
Will prove to you successful
If you'll not forget to try.
The prize is not won by the swiftest
Nor does it oft' go to the strong,
But always to the one who keeps working,
Though the path may be rough and long.

To Marjie On Her Tenth Birthday

Dear younger daughter of mine
Just arrived at the age of ten
Glad and eager, all a thrill
Another new year to begin.
Poised you stand with arms outstretched
Welcoming old Father Time.
He has ushered in another birthday,
You can never again be nine.
But we'll banish regrets as you stand today
On the edge of a brand new year
Tho' your birthdays from me will steal you away
I'll not spoil your joy with a tear.
Let me gaze in the crystal, daughter mine
To see what the year will hold
Health and happiness and the joy of work
Love and play and pleasures untold
Are mingled there. And if among them
A dragon of evil or failure you meet
You will grapple with him and slay him
And throttle him under your feet.
For back of that laughing child like face
There lies, I am glad to say
A strong will power that nothing can daunt
And a purpose that naught can dismay.
I do not fear for you, daughter mine
For your heart is loyal and true.
Just pray to God for guidance
And He will take care of you.

A Mother's Day Dialogue

Written for a Mother and Daughter Program
At Parkland Presbyterian Church. May, 1936

Marjie:

Please will you tell me, Sister dear,
The reason for this banquet, here.
It's a very queer thing, it seems to me,
That all the boys would absent be.
There were so many good things to eat,
They wouldn't want to miss such a treat.

Barbara:

I'm surprised you don't know, Marjie dear,
This is the sweetest day of all the year.
When God made the world all big and grand,
And then made people to live in the land,
They began to act like people will
And quarrel and fight, and even kill.
Then God thought, "This will never do."
"I must send some one to take care of you."
So he chose a few angels, maybe eight or ten,
And sent them down to be Mothers of men.
So since that day we have always had
Mothers. They try to keep us from being bad.
They feed us and clothe us and dry our tears,
And never stop loving us down through the years.
To show our Mothers they're appreciated
To them one day in the year is dedicated,
To show them our love and make them gay.
It's the sweetest of all times, Mother's Day.
Now what do you think we could do this year,
To show our Mother we love her dear?

Marjie:

A present would be nice of course,
Like a book, or candy, or flowers,
But I've often heard my Mother say,

41

Mother's Day (continued)

Marjie (continued):
>At times like Christmas or her birthday
>That she would rather have two good girls
>Than the costliest of diamonds or pearls.
>So let's try to be better for Mother dear,
>Not only today, but all through the year.
>'Tis a gift no one else could on her bestow.
>For that reason alone she'd like it, I know.

Barbara:
>Sh-h, here she comes.

Together:
>Most Mothers get candy, or books, or flowers,
>But these weren't good enough for ours.
>For our Mother's Day present, we give to you
>A pledge to live clean lives and true.
>To be kind and helpful and try to obey,
>Not only today, but every day.

Mother:
>You have made me happy on Mother's Day,
>Not only by the sweet things you say,
>Nor yet for the kind deeds you do,
>But mostly because I have you two.
>Though Mothers labor from dawn till eve,
>They're very happy, you may believe.
>The unhappiest woman I ever knew,
>Was one who had no work to do.
>No little ones at the close of day
>To kiss and pet and tuck away.
>A hard working Mother I may be,
>But a queen could not change places with me.
>To a Mother there's only one worthwhile.
>That one is built in the heart of her child.

Then You Came

I boasted once that one could be
Always good and strong and true
Though many lived immorally
I should be counted with the few
    Then you came.

Weak souls who erred from faithful paths
I could never quite forgive
No man could beguile me so
Though lonely I must live
    Then you came.

Love might exist, I boasted then
But I had never met him
And if I did I'd pass him by
And straightway then forget him
    Then you came.

That love should be a woman's life
I denied in merriment
Work and Home were better far
And would make her more content
    Then you came.

Perhaps you came that I might know
That Love could be Divine
And that my Destiny was controlled
By a stronger Hand than mine.

Then You Came (continued)

I only know that when you came
Love opened wide my eyes
I saw the beauties of the world
And the sunshine of the skies.

You were my world, I only lived
For a glance, a smile from you.
If I were false to love you so
Then I'd have to be untrue.

All Love to us the Bible says,
From Heaven above is sent
But if loving you is sinning
I never shall repent.

A Kiss

A kiss can be a kindly act
And never mean a thing,
Or a kiss can thrill your very soul,
And make your heart strings cling.
Kisses are no harm they say,
But no one would think that true,
If they ever got a chance
To take a kiss from you.
But could you call that harmful
That for you opens wide
The very gates of Heaven,
And leads you right inside?
The arms of death, the jaws of Hell
Would never scare me quite,
If I could share a kiss with you
With your arms about me tight.

When Lovelight Lies

When he holds me close to him
And whispers low and sighs,
Is it truth he tells to me,
Or I wonder, is it lies?
When our heartbeats sound together
And his lips are prest to mine,
Is it really love that's speaking,
Or is it — just his line?
When the lovelight from his eyes
Dim the rays of setting sun,
Is it just for me it gleams,
Or — does it shine for everyone?
Be still this doubtful heart of mine,
Take what the Gods have given.
Count each hour you spend with him,
Just one more glimpse of Heaven.
And if he loves and rides away
To find another maid,
And broken then your heart may be,
It was worth the price you paid.

I'm 'Fraid I Love You Yet

My heart keeps remembering
What I know I should forget.
Thoughts of you keep lingering,
And — I'm 'fraid I love you yet.
Soft caress and lingering glance –
Just another Summer Romance.
Wiser maiden would forget, –
But — I'm 'fraid I love you yet.
Ardent vows of love undying,
I should have known that you were lying.
Not one act do I regret,
But — I'm 'fraid I love you yet.
Lightning flash and pouring rain
Bring sweet memories back again.
Memories I would not forget —
For — I'm 'fraid I love you yet.
But I write in spite of tears
That I'm still glad that we met
If I don't see you for years and years,
Then — I'm 'fraid I'll love you yet.

True Love

The gleam of fire on Northern pine,
A starlit night, your hand on mine.
A lake asleep in kind embrace
Of moonlight beams across her face.
The sounds of night us all about.
The world we knew entire shut out.
Long silences, but minds atune.
Our very hearts can now commune.
To smooth your brow of business fret,
And watch you puff your cigarette,
Is to me a joy complete.
No other life could be so sweet.
Sound my sleep though hard the bed,
If on your shoulder lay my head.
So dared I dream of you and me.
I might have known it could not be.
Now others share that trip with you,
And do the things that I would do.
If by your side I cannot be,
You carry with you a part of me.
I wish for you, though far away,
That you enjoy just every day.
If of your life this be a sign,
That you must spend it apart from mine,
May every blessing God can give,
Rest upon you while you live.

Read Between The Lines

The great love I have hither to expressed for
you is false, and I find my indifference towards
you increases daily. The more I see you the more
you appear in my eyes, an object of contempt.
I feel myself in every way disposed and determined
to hate you. I can assure you, I have never intended
to love you, and our last conversation certainly has
left an impression on my mind, which by no means
impressed me of the high standard of your character.

If we were united I would experience nothing but the
hatred of my friends added to the everlasting dis-
pleasures of living with you. I have indeed a heart
to bestow, but I do not desire you to imagine it
at your service. I would not give it to anyone more
inconsistent and capricious than yourself and be
capable of doing justice to myself and my family.
I think that you are aware of the fact that
I speak sincerely and hope you will do me the favor of
avoiding me. You need not trouble yourself about
answering this letter as your letter would be full of
impoliteness and would not have a shadow of
wit and good sense. Believe me,
I am so converse to you that it is impossible for me
to be your loving and affectionate sweetheart.
(To be read every other line for the opposite meaning)

George's Car

Lakeview is a dandy town,
It's very clean and neat.
The people are obliging
I never saw their beat.
Of course there are no busses
And we don't have a taxi stand,
But it's not hard to get around,
If you really understand.
If you've got to go some place,
Though it be near or far,
There's not need to worry about it;
Why – Just get George's car.
If you want to go a berrying,
Or to a Ladies' Aid,
Why George's brakes are pretty bad,
But his car will make the grade.
Perhaps your girl lives out of town,
Or you're taking in the Fair,
You can just ask George, you know,
His car will get you there.
If you've got to see a doctor,
Or if you work out of town,
Why George's car will bring you up,
And probably take you down.
Of course it needs a little oil,
And it really does burn gas,

George's Car (continued)

And he says to just do fifty,
But we've got those other cars to pass.
The motor has a knock or two;
The spark plugs are pretty bad,
But when you've got to borrow a car,
It's the best that can be had.
Most always, too, about midnite,
If you hang around the inn,
George may drive it out himself,
And he's apt to say, "Hop in".
I really like this town a lot,
But I must no longer roam,
And probably I'd be worrying,
But George's car will take me home.

The Drunk

He stood at the bar in the grill room,
And he was not a pretty sight.
His eyes were wild and blood-shot
From the effects of the previous night.
His clothes were ragged and dirty.
He looked neither nice nor clean,
And you would have sworn a razor,
His face had never seen.
The noisiest man in the bar-room,
His voice rang harsh and loud,
As he jeered at every new-comer,
And cursed at the entire crowd.
I pause to watch him closely,
As he drains another mug,
And throws down a last borrowed quarter,
To pay for it with a shrug.
I know you will say, "Why bother?"
He's not worth a passing glance;
And if he's bound not to pay the piper,
Why - then, he'll probably have to dance.
Perhaps it's the humorous twinkle
That lurks in his odd brown eye.
Or mayhap, the careless wit
He throws at each passer-by.
But there's something about this drunken youth,
(He's just an overgrown lad) -

The Drunk (continued)

That seems such a waste of ability,
And I leave there feeling sad.
The world would call him lucky,
And richly blest by Fate.
He has youth, and brains, and riches,
And he's tall, and strong, and straight.
He can look fine and manly,
When he cares to take the time,
He can sing like Gabriel's angels,
And his music is divine.
He has the culture and the training
That wealth can never buy.
He bears a fine old family name,
Respected far and nigh.
If you chance to find him sober,
He has both wit and charm.
He is friendly and obliging
And just himself he'll harm.
Of course I may be wrong,
But I'll tell you what I think.
The cause of this boy's trouble
Is nothing at all but drink.
If he only would stay sober
And his friends would give him a hand,
He might stop this utter nonsense,
And really be a man.

Homeward Bound

Home to your arms, a tired bird.
My head upon your breast.
I had forgot the blessed peace
For in your arms there's rest.

As sailors say, I've been around
And trod the bonny main,
But never a moment's peace had I
'Til I came home again.

Home port you said it was
And that is how it seems,
I want to hear you sing again
Our song, "Girl Of My Dreams".

Many ventures have we had
Strange tales we could relate.
But why carry into Home Port
A lot of extra freight?

Lets dump them overboard,
And say twas yesterday
We vowed to love each other
And today's another day.

The sun is shining brightly
And stormy weather's past.
And all is well with us again
For we've got Home at last.

The American Way

"It's a cinch, I tell you", old Adolph roared,
As he plotted dirt with the Yellow Horde.
Fooled were the Japs by Hitler's lies.
They planned to take us by surprise.
Their little black eyes gave him a wink.
Together they plotted our ships to sink.

"They're nothing but playboys", Adolph said,
"Lazy and wealthy and too well fed".
The Aryans boasted, "They cannot fight".
"Their mamas won't let them out of their sight".
"Besides they're quarreling all the time".
"We think ourselves the time is prime
To surprise them by attack,
And steal upon them from the back".

They planned their moves in true Jap style.
Smirking and smiling all the while.
They didn't bother about ethics of war.
But struck from behind like the snakes they are.
They chose a Sabbath for their surprise,
As Adolph and Satan would both advise.
The results of that murder I need not tell.
Every child in America knows them well.
"Remember Pearl Harbor", a nation cries,
And now Hitler himself will get a surprise.

Mothers who had prayed for peace each night,
To keep America out of the fight,
Hastened to find their sons their caps,
And hustle them off to fight the Japs.
World War Veterans with families grown,
Said, "Come on, Son, we'd better be goin'."

The American Way (continued)

"Uncle Sam, I reckon, needs you and me
To chase this vermin into the sea.
Ma and the girls, they can make out
Till we get home, I haven't a doubt."

"I'm sorry, Coach," said the boys on the team,
And in their eyes lurked a wicked gleam,
"Without us this term you'll have to do,
We're off to kill a Jap or two."
Their coach spoke up, "The devil you say,
I joined the Air Corps yesterday."
The A.F. of L. and the C.I.O.
Looked at each other and said, "What do you know?
Come on Pals, there's a job to do.
No more strikes till we are through."
When snakes from without attack our land,
American men together stand.

America's at war. A fearful sight.
Aryans watch. Does she know how to fight?
At her helm her noble leader stands.
The fate of the world rests in his hands.
"Remember Pearl Harbor," he hears the shout.
In his clear eyes there is no doubt.
"We'll work together as we've done before,
And never fear, we'll win this war.
It will not stop till the rats are dead.
God is our witness overhead."
In those words of our leader, our motto lies;
And now it's Hitler who'll get a surprise.

A Soldier's Thought

Your father on the battlefield
Is close to you tonight.
That same moon smiles down on him
With glances just as bright.
Your father likes to feel I think
That God has put it there.
For you might need a guiding light
Without a father's care.
So as you say your prayers tonight
Close to Mother's knee,
Remember that same moon up there
Your father too can see.
He likes to think it is a sign
Put in the sky to guide us,
And help us steer our course aright,
'Till he can be beside us.
So let us pray that that same moon
Will light your father's way,
And keep him safe from all harm
Until that blessed day.

Bad Boy Butch

Bad boy Butch sat scowling
Terror of the class
Dumb at verbs and spelling
But graduate of sass.
Teacher noted more than scowl
From the corner of her eye
Saw the sad look around his mouth
Heard the hopeless sigh.
Noted the bony little frame
Beneath the dirty shirt
Wondered how so short a life
Could have been so badly hurt.
Her eyes in desperation
Sought again some way
Not to aid his nouns and spelling
But to chase his scowl away.
Fell upon a picture
Of a plane put in today
By some good boy who liked to please
In every little way.
That's the very plane, she said
How many of you knew
The one that went to Tokyo
That Jim Doolittle flew.
Gosh, teacher, spoke out Butch
I've got that at home
The teacher breathed a little prayer
Her battle was half won.

To Marjie From Mother

I must now unfold a secret
That I'd divulge to few.
For many many years, dear child
I've been deceiving you.
All those favorite dishes
That I did bake and cook
Came not from hidden talent
But from the pages of this book.
In this lies a moral
That I hope you'll ever heed
A good cook needs no genius
If she has learned to read.

(Inscribed in a gift cookbook
A Thousand Ways to Please a Husband,
copywrite, 1917)

Signs Of Spring

Along about this time of year
We watch for signs of spring
How glad we are to see the ground
Or to hear a robin sing.
But the surest sign of all the rest
Is a feeling glad and warm
That drives me out on country roads
A searching for a farm.
Most any kind of place will do
If it has a house and barn.
They all look just right to me
When I'm looking for a farm.
The family know the symptoms
And when Springtime's in the air
They look at me most sadly
And move about with care.
They just hope that I'll recover
As I've done in other years
And when I speak of trading
They try to hide their fears.
Before the sap creeps up the tree
Or they spy a blade of grass
They know I'll get the country urge
And they pray that it will pass.
There's a sale sign, I will shout
As I eagerly smell the air
Stop the car let's talk to him
And see if his terms are fair.

Signs Of Spring (continued)

Though I like just all the places
Just everywhere I look
I never yet have found one farm
That fits my pocketbook.

I've known a lot of farmers,
When age creeps on a pace
Who retire to the city
And give up the old home place.
They're tired of pigs and cattle
And feeding hens and geese
So they seek out a town house
And live a life of peace.
But when I get old and feeble
And from active duties cease
I'll hie me to the country
And end my days in peace.

Boyne City Gossip

Have you heard the latest crime wave
That's descended on our town
Sowing doubt among our members
And spreading rumors all around?

A robber lurks among us
And casts fears upon our souls
For he's not stealing gold and jewels
But snitching toilet bowls.

Right from our brand new school house
He has stolen five or six
Our whole town is in an uproar
And the School Board's got to fix.

And now the plot does thicken
For it seems the Ladies Aid
Have been meeting in the school house
And suspicions on them laid.

Gather close, I'll whisper
A new and startling clue
'Tis said the Aid's own president
Has a toilet bowl quite new.

She claims of course that it came
From somewhere down in Flint
But the Board is tracing suspects
And a bloodhounds on the scent.

And within this little city
Of at least two hundred souls
There will be no peace until we find out
Who stole those toilet bowls.

An Oration

(A Farce, written and given in Lakeview High School assembly, in honor of 'Dad Fewless, our beloved Superintendent, 1916.)

Fellow Students:

I am deeply honored this morning in being privileged to introduce to this august assembly, an important name, a name worshiped alike by Americans and Turks, by Germans and Cannibals, known from sea to sea, lisped by children, spoken reverently by gray haired philosophers, a name that brings hope to the fatherless and strikes terror to the hearts of the wicked, a name more familiar to you than either Washington or Lincoln, a name that is enshrined in the heart of every true American, and though idolized in all parts of the world, it is, I regret to say, less reverenced in his own home town. For this idol of the world, loved alike by heathen and scholar, is a citizen of your town, of little unimportant Lakeview, a town that would have remained in obscurity forever but for the knightly presence of this great man. It is needless to tell of his noble and inspiring deeds. You are familiar with them, and it would be impossible for such a humble person as I, to do them justice. With the hope that my weak effort will induce you to appreciate him more, I leave with you his name, a name that stands for Equal Suffrage, True Democracy, Peace with all nations and a school room devoid of note writing, gum chewing, paper wads, rubber balls, rolling marbles, baby ribbon acts, courting sessions, Ladies' Aid Societies and Y.M.C.A. meetings, the greatest name in all the world and the one most dear to us —

T.H. Fewless.

My Last Will And Testament

(Written while in college after being told that we would have a test in Anglo-Saxon on the following day. Dr. Brown and our class had played for weeks instead of study. To prepare for the test in one night was impossible. I spent the time writing my will. It served a purpose for someone gave it to Dr. Brown and he postponed the test.)

Knowing or surmising that I tomorrow must meet my death at the hand of Dr. Brown in punishment for my ignorance of all Anglo-Saxon declensions, I hereby, upon this 16th night of January, in the year of Our Lord, 1919, being sane and in my right mind, do compose this last will and testament.

To my patient teacher and stern executor, Dr. Brown, I bequeath my scanty knowledge of Anglo-Saxon which may be of some slight use in the composition of his Anglo-Saxon grammar.

To my beloved sister, I bequeath my untidy hair. May she succeed in arranging it neatly. In life, my failure to do so did sorely grieve her.

To my roomate I bequeath my knowledge of French in order that she may the more intelligently correspond with her friend "overseas".

To Forest Averill, I bequeath my knowledge of the French Revolution.

To Herbert D. Ver Veer, I bequeath my religious devotion, my belief in Methodism, my love for Tennyson's "Princess", and my right to vote.

To my fellow student teacher, Glenda Doxey, I bequeath my talent to bluff with the caution to use it wisely. It caused my death.

I beg leave to make the following requests:

Burn my Anglo-Saxon Grammar in order that it cannot haunt my friends.

When my head has fallen like famous Danton, I ask that it may be held up to the class. It's worth it.

Upon my tombstone engrave these words:
"Innocent, tho' stupid, she met her fate
By not studying the Declensions until too late."

A Country School House

I am going, today, on an imaginary visit, to the country school which I attended when a little girl. If the reader is so inclined, he may accompany me, the only necessary equipment being a tin dinner pail. At least, that is all the girls ever bring. The boys are different, they come barefooted and with their pockets full of beans and corn to throw at the teacher or at each other.

The last bell is ringing as we approach and it is great fun to see the boys and girls scamper in from the playground. Now all is quiet and we are free to observe the building itself. It faces the south and is about eighteen feet wide and thirty feet long. It is painted a pure white, a color which makes a striking contrast with the blue green woods on the eastern and northern sides, and the smooth, well-kept grounds surrounding the building. There are two doors in the front of the house with cement steps leading up to them and little cement porches. Between these is a bay window. These doors open into halls, one for the boys and one for the girls. We will enter one of them and look around us. In one corner is a row of shelves full of dinner pails, and if it is in the boy's side we will find their caps here, just as they threw them when they made a wild dash for the school room. There are rows of books on one side of the hall and a wash-stand in the other corner, on which rests a tin wash-basin and a pail of water which is always empty. The thirst of country school children is never quenched and "Teacher may I get a drink?", is the most common of all requests. Above the stand hangs a mirror, and after smoothing our hair, we enter the school-room proper. Directly in front of us is the teacher's desk, with books and papers neatly arranged, - country school teachers are nearly always neat -, and a vase of wild flowers beside them.

Back of the desk is a high, straight-backed chair, which, partly because of its uncomfortable lines, and partly because of the unceasing

A Country School House (continued)

duties of the teacher, is seldom occupied. Near the bay-window in front is the organ, and above it is draped a large United States flag. In the north-west corner of the room are two book cases. One contains all the novels of Scott and Dickens, "Pilgrims' Progress", Owen Meredith's "Lucille", Blackmore's "Lorna Doone", Louise May Alcott's books, "Arabian Nights", Grimm's and Anderson's "Fairy Tales", and a few other books. The other case is full of encyclopedias and text books. On the top of this is the Globe. In the north east corner of the room is a stove. Above the blackboards which extend around the entire room, are pictures most of them portraits of famous men. There we find Christopher Columbus, George Washington, Abraham Lincoln, Ulysses Grant, Admiral Dewey and Francis Willard. The only other picture is a painting of Sir Galahad and his horse.

There are three windows on each side of the room, the person who planned the building, evidently not knowing that the light in a school room should come from one side only. The seats are double and run north and south, there being four rows of them. The desks are painted dark red with little ink wells on top that have covers. These covers are favorite playthings with the pupils and the majority of the ink wells are used for paper-wad receptacles. The seats are painted yellow and two pupils sit at every desk. Between these rows of seats and the teacher's desk, are the recitation seats, two long yellow seats, extending entirely across the room.

Now that we have noted the room and its furniture, let us take a seat among the students and watch them at their work.

The Land Of His Dreams

Things had gone wrong with Percy. In fact things generally did seem to go wrong with him. The trouble was, he thought, as he flung himself down in the hammock, no one appreciated him nor the things he did, here at the Normal. One would expect to find fairly intelligent people at a Normal School and Percy had searched diligently. But although there were a great many ready to discuss the war and baseball, no one seemed to care for Browning, nor be vitally interested in evolution. If Percy asked a co-ed's opinion of Emerson's "Oversoul", she would begin to rave about Alan Seegar's poems, or Empey's "Over The Top". Wordsworth was cast aside, Shakespeare left unread, while volumes of "Blood and Thunder" books on the war and life in "No Man's Land", were devoured with eagerness. Civilization was being ruined; culture and an appreciation of fine art was becoming extinct and Percy St. Clair lay in the hammock and bemoaned his fate.

The men were bad enough but those girls—! Percy gave a snort of disgust. The latest craze was Woman Suffrage and those girls were sending a petition to the Senate asking that they might be given their rights, the ballot. The folly of it, the insanity of such a proposal. It was preposterous.

Of course girls never worried Percy. Some men found them amusing, but as yet he had found no desire for such recreation. His spare time was spent in libraries, delving among old books, — Carlyle and Shakespeare. Their society, there for, had satisfied him absolutely. He had no time to spend with frivolous young ladies whose minds were too small to understand any subject other than the latest song, or the newest fashion. But Peggy Dennis really had seemed fairly intelligent. She had appeared interested in his young philosophy when he had condescended to impart it to her, and though he had often thought a great deal of it was over her head, she made bright comments which showed she thought about such things herself. One day though, to Percy's great surprise, she had confessed a dislike for Browning. He had come upon her unexpectedly and found her knitting her brows over one of Browning's poems. When she saw him she threw the book down and exclaimed petulantly, "Why did he leave half the words out of that thing? It's like a lecture taken down in Shorthand." Percy then explained to her that it was just that in

The Land Of His Dreams (continued)

Browning that revealed his superiority of mind. He added that it took a person with some intelligence to appreciate such poetry, and in thinking it over afterwards he wondered why Peggy got angry.

But though her mind was narrow she was a pretty nice sort of girl, he thought, so maybe "he'd fix things up". His generous intentions was forgotten next morning when he entered the Normal. There at a table, to his disgust, sat Peggy, her head visible over a large placard, bearing the words, "Petition for Woman Suffrage". He knew she saw him but her slightly elevated nose was the only indication she gave of his presence.

All these grievances flitted through Percy's mind as he lay in the hammock and each one made him just that much more dissatisfied with the world in which he lived. "How wonderful it would be", he sighed, "to dwell in a place where peoples' minds were big enough and broad enough to appreciate the great things of life, and where baseball games, Woman Suffrage and war were left to people of less intelligence."

But there was no use of one thinking about it. There was no such "Utopia" on this earth and in utter weariness, Percy rolled over in the hammock and went to sleep.

PART II

Everywhere was fog, dense and gloomy, and an unearthly quietness. One could not see far in such an atmosphere, but dark mountains loomed on either side, and Percy could feel their cold, rocky exteriors when he stretched out his hands. There was no sunlight nor no starlight, nothing but a horrible, heavy darkness pressing in from all sides.

Percy had just reached the moon and he found it very hard to travel about. He had hoped to stumble upon a village or farm house (he supposed they had farm houses here), but he had groped along in the darkness for along time now, and had found no trace of habitation.

Percy was hungry; a strange sensation for him. He had never worried about food on the earth but now he wondered where his supper was coming from. That must not stop him now, though. He kept on moving in the slow, groping way which the darkness made

The Land Of His Dreams (continued)

necessary.

Percy shivered. How chilly it was here on the moon. He thought of the warm fire in his room at home and sighed. Then he remembered how he had been misunderstood there, and resolutely pushed on again.

Percy was tired. His feet ached and he wanted to lie down. He was not accustomed to exercise and his strength was failing rapidly, but on he went.

At last he could go no further. He sank down against the cold, hard rock, and fatigue and despair overpowered him. And he was beginning to feel afraid. If this was the moon it was a weird, uncanny place. And it was as cold as a vault. He thought of Browning's poetry. He began to recite it, but the well loved lines brought no solace now. Lines from Shakespeare came to his mind, but their charm was gone. It was food and warmth he wanted, not poetry and philosophy. He had a vague idea that perhaps this was the way Empey felt after going through No Man's Land. Small wonder he wrote the kind of book he did, Percy thought. There seemed to be a common bond between him now and those men over there. It was true there were no shells bursting round him but could anything be more dreadful than this darkness?

He put his face in his hands and groaned aloud. Just then a hollow voice said, "Come with me," and a cold clammy hand grasped his. Percy could not see the speaker, but he heard a click and felt a door recede in the mountain against which he leaned. The person—if person it was—still grasping his hand in a cold clutch, led him through the door. It swung behind him. Again he heard the click and shuddered. Now they were ascending a flight of stairs, steep and narrow with mountain rock on either side. It was darker than ever here and Percy blindly followed his guide; higher and higher, though he knew not where they were going. He began to think the stairs would never end. His guide uttered no word, though he still grasped him with that cold, clammy hand. Percy was afraid. The whole thing was uncanny. He wondered if it was not some spirit leading him, some strange phantom of the moon. The feel of that hand filled him with horror. His heart seemed to freeze within him and he shuddered.

The Land Of His Dreams (continued)

Would the horrible journey never end? Where was he being taken? He did not care much. Nothing could be worse than this.

His guide stopped, released his hand and a door was pushed open before him. "The Princess Theodosia", said the hollow voice. Half blinded by an unaccustomed light, Percy stood staggering in the doorway. Then his vision cleared. A strange sight met his eyes. The room was high and lofty. Walls, ceiling and floor were all of rock. In the walls were cut small windows which let in the light. There was no fog here, it was too high up for that but there was no sunlight either. The room was gloomy and bare, with the chilly, penetrating dampness of a vault. It was well furnished, but there were no carpets, nor curtains, no luxurious chairs, no soft cushions, and no warm fire. There were straight hard chairs and thousands of books on shelves which completely surrounded three sides of the room. On the fourth side was an iron throne and from it descended the Princess Theodosia. She came toward him, book in hand; she was extremely tall and slender and she seemed to glide rather than walk. She was clothed in sombre grey which seemed to Percy to be made from a piece of the fog, through which he had just come. Her hair was a pale yellow, her eyes large and sombre, the color of her dress. Her face was as white and stony as marble and her forehead broad and high. It was as if a stone image stood before him, so colorless and lifeless did she seem. Percy thought of the dancing eyes of earthly Peggy and sighed. The Princess extended a white hand. It was cold and clammy like the atmosphere. A chill crept up his spine. She spoke in a cold, uncanny voice and bade him welcome to the moon kingdom. It sounded more like a funeral pnell than a greeting and Percy shuddered again. Then he glanced at the book in her hand and his spirits rose. It was a volume of Browning's poetry. She led him to the throne and they ascended it together. The Princess opened the book and began to read. How well she interprets that, thought Percy. At last he had reached a land where Browning's poetry, five thousand leagues above earthly minds could be understood. Was he satisfied? The Princess rang for food. A little moon dwarf appeared bearing a tray of green cheese, soda crackers, cucumber salad, and ice cream. Percy wondered if this was considered a substantial meal by the moon people and unconsciously

The Land Of His Dreams (continued)

he gave his old snort of disgust. She looked at him with such cold curiosity that the color rushed to his face. At once he was ashamed. What if there were no color, warmth, nor food here; there was intellectuality. Was not that what he had longed for? He turned from the food after a pretense of eating and began a discussion of Browning. What a wonderful mind the Princess had. At last he had found his equal. When Browning was exausted they turned to others. Percy was almost happy. Then there were the books. All the old master pieces were here and not one volume of Alan Seegar nor one line of Private Pete.

But somehow, Percy was not satisfied. He was cold and lonely. He wanted companionship and food and life. For the first time in his life he wished for a newspaper and most of all he longed for Peggy. He had found intellectuality at last, only to discover that that alone did not satisfy. He wanted warmth and color, life and love, and he could not find them here. He was tired of Browning and longed for the earth again.

The Princess turned her sombre eyes upon him. She saw what was the matter and brought him a field glass. "Oh earth friend," said she, "you long for home, you are not contented. Perhaps when you view the earth through these you will be glad to stay." Her cold voice filled him with forboding. He grasped the glass and focused it upon the earth. Oh how nice it looked, how warm and sunny and cheerful. It fairly glowed with life and color. At last he saw his own country. Then he singled out the Normal. Down the steps came Peggy. How wonderful she was, but stay! Who was by her side? Gay Jimmie Wilson and she was smiling up at him. "Oh why did I leave," cried Percy, "what is intellectuality, what is science when Peggy is gone," and he threw the glasses from him angrily.

PART III

"Why throw brickbats at me?" a gay voice called. Percy awoke and rubbed his eyes. On the steps stood Jimmie Wilson; at his feet the book Percy had just thrown. Remembering his dream, Percy grinned sheepishly and welcomed his friend.

The Armistice;
Comparisons and Interpretations

The greatest war in the history of the world has drawn to a satisfactory close. Germany and the things Germany stood for have been defeated, and as her armies are beaten back to their own country, their vanishes the system of autocracy from the face of the earth.

Europe today is a hot bed of Revolution. As we look over the continent and see the all apparent results of the war, - devastated Belgium, worn-out France, Russia, seething with anarchy and revolt, disbanded and dissolved Austria Hungary, Germany humiliated and defeated, it is hard to think the world, - the people of all nations - have triumphed against an enemy. But such is indeed the case.

The French Revolution was a period of crime, of misery, of unbelievable horrors, but all this is forgotten in the grand results which it brought forth. It *tried* to make the world safe for democracy. We have accomplished it.

The French Revolution ushered in a new era but the European Revolution, now in progress, is ushering in a new world. We Americans, with our old traditional policy, of a government of the people, by the people, and for the people, together with England, who early recognized the rights of mankind by her "Magna Charta"; France, with a revolution to her credit, and with our other allies, who have come through one way or another, to believe in the rights of man, have won the victory. We have made the world safe for democracy, and the abdications in Russia, Germany, and Bulgaria are merely proving this to be so. Practically a whole continent has been delivered from under the "yoke of a tyrant".

Autocracy is crushed, Kaiserism and all the things the name implies, have fought their last battle.

The future is before us and the future can be anything the nations choose to make it. The Armistice gives us some knowledge of what this future is to be. The terms of it are severe, but just and very necessary. They are intended to be the prelude of a permanent peace, and as such, they must do away with the enemy of peace - namely autocracy.

It is like the treatment of a wound. First every particle of the

Armistice (continued)

infected tissue must be skillfully removed by the surgeon and then a cleansing fluid is sent into the most hidden recesses of the infected parts. The result is a quick and complete healing.

Mankind has suffered a grievous but not incurable wound. The armistice is our treatment of it. After the military authorities have completed their skillful work, and after the streams of democracy have been allowed to flow into the farthest recesses of the diseased government, after the military autocracy which caused the war, has been destroyed, there comes a new social order, a restored and healthy society of nations who will endeavor to attain liberty, happiness, and prosperity for all mankind.

With these things in mind, the terms of the armistice were formed. Severe they may be but if Germany is ever a democracy she must submit to the surgeon's knife. Germany cannot find fault because the terms of the armistice are identically the same terms that she imposed upon France at the close of the Franco–Prussian war. The wording in most places is exactly the same. Of course there are a few differences due to the changes in time as for instance "cessation of operations by land and in the air". But at the time of the Franco-Prussian war "operations in the air" had not begun, so this difference can be overlooked.

So if Germany, herself, has approved of the terms of the armistice, we should not find fault. President Wilson wisely saw that Marshall Foch, who is in the best position to understand the nature of the wound, should administer the treatment.

The following brief summary of this treatment shows the keen foresight of the surgeon: "Germany must accept literally, the fourteen peace terms laid down by President Wilson's message of January, the eighth, which includes the righting of the wrong done to France in 1871, in Alsace-Lorraine, the creation of an independent Polish state out of the territory inhabited by indisputable Polish population; the evacuation and restoration of Belgium to independence; the readjustment of the frontiers of Italy, "recognizing the lines of nationality" which means giving the Italian portions of Austria-Hungary back to Italy, the restoration of Rommania, Serbia, and Monte negro, the freest opportunity for the people of Austria-Hungary

Armistice (continued)

to obtain "autonomous development", the evacuation of all territory belonging to Russia, and the destruction of all impediments to the free development of the democracy, and guarantees that the national armaments will be reduced. The Central Powers must withdraw "everywhere" from invaded territory before the terms of an armistice are even proposed. Germany must eliminate her present autocratic government and set up a government whose word can be trusted and who can be the spokesman of the free and untrammeled will of the people of Germany, a real democracy that can be accepted in the League of Nations. Within fourteen days Germany is to evacuate all invaded territory. Belgium, France, Alsace Lorriane, and Luxenburg. All inhabitants of these countries are to be restored at once. The German armies must withdraw from a considerable stretch of German territory on the left or west bank of the Rhine. The Allies are to hold this ground and they are to hold the bridgeheads on the other side of the Rhine, opposite this territory.

On the east bank of the Rhine, there is to be a neutral zone, twenty five miles in width on an average. All this German territory must be free from German troops within twenty five days.

The Allied garrisons are to hold all fortified points on the west side of the Rhine. No destruction or injury to people must be permitted during the evacuation, under the threat of reprisal. Military stores, equipment, etc. must be handed over to the Allies intact. The position of all mines or poisoned wells must be indicated.

Germany must hand over to the Allies, five thousand pieces of artillery, (twenty five hundred heavy and twenty five hundred field), thirty thousand machine guns, two thousand aeroplanes, five thousand locomotives, fifty thousand wagons, ten thousand motor trucks. Railroads and other material, including bridges, telephones, and coal in the evacuated territory, must be given up intact.

All submarines must be given up. Six battle cruisers, eight light cruisers, ten battleships, and fifty destroyers must be disarmed and interned.

The Allied war and merchant ships must have free access to the Baltic. The Russian vessels in the Black Sea, seized by Germany, must be handed over to the Allies. The right of trading with the Allies is

Armistice (continued)

assured to all neutral countries, while on the other hand, the right of blockading the German ports is retained by the Allies. All allied civilians, interned or deported, must be surrendered within a month and reparation for damage made. The former treaties imposed upon Russia and Rommania by Germany are to be abandoned. Not only the German troops, but also the "German instructors, prisoners, and civilians as well as the military agents" now in Russia, are to be recalled. Germany must withdraw her troops from Turkey and Rommania at once. The duration of the armistice is for thirty days.

The terms of the Armistice with Austria-Hungary are much like those with Germany. Half of the artillery must be surrendered to the Allies, the Austrian army must be demobilized, all invaded territory must be evacuated and this territory shall be occupied by the Allied troops, allied prisoners of war must be released, fifteen submarines, and all German submarines which are in or may hereafter enter Austro-Hungarian territorial waters must be surrendered to the Allies. All other submarines are to be completely disarmed.

All warships not surrendered to the Allies by the terms of the armistice are to be concentrated in Austro-Hungarian naval bases designated by the Allies, where they are to be completely disarmed. Freedom of navigation to all warships and merchant ships of the allied powers to be given in the Adriatic and up to the Danube river and in the territorial waters of Austria-Hungary.

The existing blockade of Austro-Hungarian ports is to remain unchanged. The Allies are to have the right of free movement over all road and rail and waterways in Austria-Hungary. By these terms Austria-Hungary is practically converted into an Ally for the Allies are able to use her railroads, warships, and territory against Germany. The same is true in the cases of Bulgaria and Turkey. The most important consequences of the armistice with Turkey, is that it opens up the Dardenelles, the Casparian and the Black Sea to the British and French navies so the latter will be able to send aid to Russia and to destroy the German power in the Black Sea.

There is scarcely a country in Europe that is not affected by these armistices.

As we look at the map of the continent we can see alterations in

Armistice (continued)

the boundary lines of nearly every nation. France has gained Alsace-Lorraine, ruthlessly torn from her in 1871 by the Prussian government, "Italia Irredenta" has been restored again to Italy, the land of Belgium is at last free of the Hun; Germany has less territory than she had in 1914.

But it is in Austria-Hungary where the remarkable change has taken place. She has been completely dissolved.

Our recognition of the independence of the Checko-Slavs heralded the death of Austria-Hungary. Twelve little nations, owing their independence to nature herself have sprung up. Of all these people, the most interesting are the Poles. In the middle ages, their country was more powerful than Russia. Her territory reached from the Black Sea to the Baltic, from the Oder to the Dnieper. But in the last portion of the 18th century, it was cooly divided between Russia, Prussia and Austria. Russia took 7,000,000 people, Prussia and Austria, 3,000,000 a piece. The story of these people, the crimes committed against them, the torture inflicted upon them, their suppression and subugation forms one of the blackest chapters in history. But now she is free. The world is safe for democracy and Poland can again be an independent Nation.

At first it appears almost brutal to propose the extinction of one of the great powers of Europe. But a little thought upon the subject will do away with such qualms. Austria-Hungary is no nation at all. She never has been one and never will be one. It is merely the product of a series of political crimes, extending over centuries, and its existance is a constant challenge to democracy and freedom. It has risen on the dead bodies of other nations, it has grown by plundering its subjects and by suppressing by the most inhuman of methods, all the instincts and ambitions of free men. It's death means that these people may come to life.

The king of Bulgaria has abdicated and Germany is involved in a Revolution, the first one to her credit in the history of the world. But so far we cannot tell whether this Revolution is based upon a genuine change of heart or upon fear and hatred.

President Wilson said when he presented the terms of the armistice to Congress, "The people who have just come out from

Armistice (continued)

under the yoke of arbitrary government, and who are now coming at last into their freedom, will never find the treasures of liberty they are in search of, if they look for them by the light of the torch. They will find that every pathway that is stained with the blood of their own brothers, leads to the wilderness and not to the seat of their hope". But the fact remains that "kaiserism" has vanished from Germany and she now has the privilege and we hope the desire, to establish a government which shall derive its powers from the consent of the governed.

One result of the armistice is that the Allies must change their policy toward Russia. Thus far it has been necessary and advisable that our force should act as a means of protection for Russia, against the Central Power and herself. We have stood for "autonomous development" and we must now leave Russia alone to work out her own government. Of course we might do it much better and more wisely than she, but we are not Russians. We have no just reason to remain longer in Russia.

If the terms of the armistice are made the foundations for the peace terms, the second one of President Wilson's fourteen points may entirely revolutionize the sea policy of the world. I say "may" for already the Allies have intimated that they cannot accept this term unless interpreted in a certain way. It is as follows: "Absolute freedom of navigation upon the seas, outside of territorial waters, alike in peace and in war, except as the seas may be closed in whole or in part, by international convenants". "Freedom of the seas", the Allies point out, is open to various interpretations, some of which they could not accept. They must therefore reserve to themselves complete freedom on this subject when they enter the peace conference". Since the beginning of our history, the United States has maintained that "free ships make free goods". It has desired to extend to the high seas the same laws which serve to protect private properties in invaded countries. The Allies object to this.

America entered the war, not only to help put an end to autocracy, but to protect its right on the seas. So we have a very real interest in the forth coming discussion relating to Clause 2.

The greatest of all the results of the Armistice will be the League

Armistice (continued)

of Nations.

This is the direct aim of Peace - to create a league of free nations in which hatreds and antagonisms (whether social or national) will have nothing to feed on and will disappear. In this league of nations there must be a common bond of sympathy and understanding, which will make the world safe for the small nations as well as the large ones. In this league, Germany will have her place. She cannot be kept in a madhouse as one article put it. Whatever we have said to the contrary, the Germans are people, and we cannot ostracize them.

During the war we encouraged a spirit of pugnacity but it is now out of place. Our first duty as a member of the League of Nations, is to be generous and just toward our alien enemies. We must accomplish this before that league can be a success.

The war is over and our democracy has stood the test. We have proved that America, the "melting pot" of all nationalities is so constituted that she cannot fail. Wilhelm proved to be a false prophet as well as a false leader and once again right in the guise of Democracy triumphed over wrong.

An English Drama

There are many dark pages in the records of England, but the darkest of all reigns, historians seem to agree, fell in the fifteenth century.

For three hundred years war had thrown its dark cloud over the land unbroken by the welcome presence of peace. The cruel reason for this was the Medieval kings feared peace, feeling that the only way to keep control within their kingdom was to rage war with foreign countries. But we have only to study the pages of the history of the 15th century to find the falseness of this policy, for it was in this age that Religious Massacres reached their height; that kings were imprisoned and cruelly treated before they were beheaded. That young heirs to the throne were murdered and the country literally ran with blood. Perhaps the coldest blooded of all these kings and certainly the most miserly was Henry the VII of England.

He had managed to gain the throne by having his successor, equally as wicked, put to death, and had amassed a huge fortune by wresting the hard earned coins from the hands of poor peasants. Another successful way of accumulating money had been to have wealthy nobles and their families put to death and confiscate their fortunes. He was cruel to his queen, cold and unkind to his children, he had no friends and never in his wicked life had he been known to have done one unselfish deed.

His Queen, Elizabeth, on the other hand was sweet and charitable. Daughter of a former English King, she had been kept in prison with her lady mother; had witnessed the murder of her young brother, heir to the throne, and had early learned what it meant to be poor and friendless. In the beginning of her married life she had attempted to implore the King on her knees to be more merciful to his subjects, only to be pushed aside by her cruel husband. After this she had confined her prayers to her own chamber but never did she cease to pray for the needy and persecuted, and also for the soul of the king.

Never having performed a kindness in his life, the king had no conception of unselfish love. He went on his cold, selfish way, his chief joy being in counting his gold, and waging war upon people at home and abroad.

The Queen despaired of ever touching his cruel heart, but one

An English Drama (continued)

night her prayers were answered.

The King had a dream and it left him much troubled.

He quickly summoned the Counsellor of the Kingdom, a great and wise man, dear to the hearts of the English people. Although the King seldom heeded his advice, (much to the sorrow of England), he respected his wisdom and eagerly turned to him now to interpret his dream:

Oh, Counsellor, last night as I reclined upon my bed, sleep had scarce touched my eye lids when a most horrible apparition came to disturb my slumber. This figure appeared to be a monstrous giant, more fearful and ugly than words can describe, who breathed forth fire and scattered destruction before him. The bravest of our peasant soldiers fled or fell dead at sight of him but the most horrible part of my story is still to relate. I saw beautiful fairy-like figures come dancing in and each in turn introduced themselves to me. Innocence, Peace, Religion, Prosperity, Love and Pity were there and each in turn was killed or frightened away by this terrible giant. Then I saw our race of honest peasants pass away and all who survived this creature became in turn giants of horrible appearance and great stature who preyed upon each other. Law and Order passed away and in place of my people was an inhuman race who heeded neither king nor God but lived for their own lust and gain. Oh, Counsellor, interpret this terrible nightmare that depresses my very soul.

While the King thus spoke, a sweet expression came to the countenance of the good old counsellor, as if he were thanking God for this visitation. As the King finished he turned to him and replied:

Your Majesty, though my words should anger you I shall speak frankly. Your dream is truly a Divine Warning and the meaning of it is clear. For years you have lived a life of greed and selfishness. You have levied taxes and collected money with never a thought of the sacrifice of your people. Then you have gloated over those coins wrested from the peasants and sent them forth to be killed in unnecessary wars that you might obtain more glory. The giant, oh, King, is none other than you who is fast destroying the virtues of your people by your cruel deeds.

The King was really to be pitied as he sat on his throne a dejected

An English Drama (continued)

figure with his head on his hands.

Oh, Counsellor, I own the truth of your words, but in the whole kingdom there is not a more wretched, unhappy figure than I. I would trade all my gold for peace of mind, and one night's rest.

The good old Counsellor, who had seen other kings come and go, and knew their weaknesses, was touched.

"Your Majesty, never in your life have you done one unselfish act. You have missed the glow of happiness that comes through love and service. If you wish happiness you must learn the secret of it from your betters. Send forth your messengers and call to your aid all those through out the kingdom who have learned the joy of service.

The King, who in his desperation, was ready to grasp at anything to find peace of mind, called unto him four most trustworthy messengers, and commanded them to search dilligently throughout the kingdom until they found four people who had performed the most acts of unselfishness and love.

So now if you will accompany me we will visit a humble dwelling, the home of a kind, old peasant woman, who is eagerly awaiting the return of her stalwart son from his day's work, is standing at the window with her hand over her eyes, anxiously peering into the distance to catch a glimpse of his approach.

This woman whom we see is good Dame Margaret who has reared her son to fear God and love his King. From early dawn until late at night these two honest people toil, and never have they uttered one word of complaint against the heavy demands of their sovereign. Grateful that they are able to keep the necessities of life, the old peasant mother never forgets to pray each day for their King and send to him the choicest gifts of their harvest. Only one thought mars the content of her kindly old heart and makes her fairly quake with fear. That is the dread that some day her strong, brave son will be called forth to fight for the King. But she faces this with courage and resignation. If called her son must respond to duty.

We see the mother turn briskly from the window and pass to the hearth. Her quick journeys between the hearth and the little table, covered by a snowy cloth, tell us her son is approaching. Now his step sounds on the the threshold and the mother's face lights up as his

An English Drama (continued)

stalwart form appears.

After greeting his mother, the young man begins excitedly:

Oh, Mother, I had the most wonderful experience this day. On my way home through the woods I heard a cry for help. Rushing down a side path, I came upon a young noble man, who had been unmounted from his steed, while engaged in a struggle with a fierce wild boar. I approached very cautiously, took my axe and killed the boar. The young nobleman was so grateful for my service he begged me to go with him to his great castle and live with him as a fellow nobleman.

The mother rejoices in her son's good fortune and urges him to go, although the separation is breaking her heart.

While he is telling her that he will never never leave her a knock sounds upon the door.

Now we return to Henry's court where great excitement prevails.

The King's page, a great favorite of the Queen, enters bearing joyful tidings, for lo', the first messenger has returned from his long search and not in vain. In triumph he ushers in a Crusader, whose saintly countenance is recognized by many members of the court. This is good St. George whose life has been spent in the service of his people. His name has come down through the ages as England's Patron Saint of Service.

Scarce has he been welcomed when the second messenger appears accompanied by the familiar and well loved figure of Robin Hood, who has spent much of his life in fighting for the rights of the common people. As his graceful figure, clad in forest green, is kneeling before the King, the third messenger arrives.

With him is a doctor whose scholarly presence forcibly reminds King Henry of the feeble ray of Science Medicine trying to keep alive in England and his own indifference to it in the past. He bids the aged man arise but before he can make amends, the last messenger of all is heard in the outer court.

Of all the knights his journeys have been the longest and most fatiguing but his patience was rewarded, for with him we see the old peasant mother and her son, their faces fairly radiating kindness and self-sacrifice. As they prostrate themselves before the much loved

An English Drama (continued)

King for whom they have often prayed, the Counsellor remembers the words of Jesus, "He that is least among you the same shall be great." But more marvelous than this, the King, himself, stoops to assist the peasant woman to arise. Then he faces the court. Scarce needed they, his up raised hand to quiet them. They stand as people entranced, gazing upon the changed countenance of their lord and master. Can this face, transfigured with love and gratitude be that of their grasping King? And then in words of deepest contrition, the King speaks to them, acknowledging freely his wrongs of the past, fervently thanking the good old Counsellor and these honored visitors for showing him the errors of his ways and promising to be kind and considerate in the future. Then to cheer his master the Jester enters and amuses the court with his antics.

Now that evil is avoided and there is cause for rejoicing the King summons his merry Dancers who perform the Stick Dance.

The monarch blesses his court, and with his Queen, then descend from the throne and kneel among his people.

America's Debt To The Negro

All thinking Americans today agree that one of the major post war problems we are going to have to cope with is that age old question of the Negro and his social status in our country.

Several problems seem to have come to a head during our generation. For instance, the Japanese menace. I can remember, and so can you if you are in your thirties or older, how like a shadow on the wall, the Far East, for several decades, has been lurking there in darkness, waiting for someone to throttle him. People said some day he would have to be reckoned with, and we pictured it as being hundreds of years away. Well, it happened that he chose to rise up during our time, and so did the hated Nazi. Our generation said, "Fine. Let them come. Let's really polish off these rats and clean the world up, once and for all, so our children and their children can have a chance." No one, now, doubts but what it is going to be done thoroughly. No more half way jobs for us.

It seems too bad, in a way, that when our heroes return from the battlefields of the world, weary and foot sore and ill, before they can really rest, they will need to clean up a few things at home. Foremost among these, is the Negro Problem.

I, for one, am glad they will be the ones to do it. Having rubbed shoulders with all the peoples of the earth, they will be able to contemplate a black brother without shuddering or drawing back, for fear of being contaminated, as, I regret to say, many so called Americans now do. They will have met the Negro in army camps, fought by his side on the battle field, shared with him a hospital ward, and they will have learned, I hope, that color is truly only "skin deep", and we are all brothers at heart.

The problem of the Negro child lies very close to my heart, because I have spent eighteen years teaching him, along with forty-one other nationalities, in one of Michigan's industrial cities.

I remember when I first signed a contract to teach in this school, my father was greatly perturbed. Having been born and raised in the South, he shared their prejudice of the Negro. He instructed me to refuse to have one in my class. Now, I hold a very high respect for my father and usually obeyed him implicitly, but this was one of the times I chose to use my own judgment. In fact, not that first year, nor any

America's Debt To The Negro (continued)

other year did I ever have a desire to send a Negro child out of class. Other nationalities among those forty-two gave me more trouble, by far, though I won't mention which ones. I liked them all, and found before long that school problem cases could not be classified by nationality nor color. All races have their good and bad.

Then, too, in that very first home room of mine, I found Timothy. I must take time to tell you about him, because if it had not been for that young Negro boy, I would not, now be writing this article.

In the junior high school in which I taught there was an enrollment of better than two thousand. Each teacher was given a home room of forty odd boys and girls, for whom she was to be responsible for a three year period. She met with them each morning for thirty minutes, took the attendance, read the Bible, advised and corrected them as need be, and sent them off to classes. There was always a great many things to be done in the short time alloted, and, that first year, the dread of leaving some important task undone used to terrify me. I was lucky, though, in having drawn a home room that had already been in the school one term. Seeing I was young and inexperienced and frightened, they at once assumed the responsiblity of looking after me. They did a fine piece of work getting me started and "teaching me the ropes", even at first guiding me about the huge building as I was afraid of getting lost. They were 7A's and a fine group of boys and girls. Their president was Timothy, a handsome, intelligent Negro boy, for whom they all had the greatest respect. He took charge of the business meeting that first morning, and also of me. Never have I had any school principal show more poise, courtesy, and understanding than did that Negro boy.

I learned, afterwards, that his mother was a cultured, refined woman from Virginia and his uncle was a lawyer in Detroit. Once, later on in our acquaintance, he told me I reminded him of his mother. I still treasure that remark as one of the highest compliments any student ever paid me. I've always regretted that I never met her. She had given her boy excellent training in two qualities that helped make him successful—namely, courtesy and cleanliness.

His manners were a part of him, not just put on on occasions as those of most boys I've worked with in school. Timothy never failed to rise when an older person entered, and always opened doors, pulled out chairs, and picked up objects with the ease and dexterity of a trained English butler. To watch him, one could not help but know he practiced those manners at home.

Now, don't get the idea he was humble and fawning in his attitude, because such was not the case. His manner was as noble and dignified as that of a young prince. Three times in the period I knew him, did I see him lose his self control.

The first time was in a ninth grade English class when a school bully had started to walk out of the room when I had refused him permission. Before I could interfere, Timothy had leaped to his feet and ordered him back to his seat in no uncertain terms. At the time, I fairly gloated over the incident, that although black, he had within him the qualities of leadership, and would be found on the side of justice.

The second time Timothy lost his dignity was a much different type of situation. This happened when he was a 9A and about ready to leave our building for senior high school. He had in the meantime become one of the leaders of the school. Besides being the vice president of the student council, (the first Negro child to attain such an honor in our building), he was president of his home room, of several clubs, one of the leading athletes in the city, a splendid orator, having won one state ribbon, and above all, an A student in all of his classes. He was a leader of his own race, highly respected by the white children, and a close friend of many of his teachers. In spite of all this honor he remained unspoiled.

Though always respectful, he never acted inferior to the white race as many Negro children do in their attempt to get along. He had several good friends among the white boys, but he treated the girls with a deference that was pleasant to see and discouraged any too friendly advances on their part. Children, as a whole, I have noticed, unless prejudiced and coerced by elders, are democratic and naturally friendly. Timothy gratefully accepted this friendship from his own sex, but his own sense of propriety made him aloof with the girls.

In his class was a beautiful little coquette, sophisticated beyond her years, who would have flirted with her own grandfather. For some unaccountable reason, she began showering her attentions upon

America's Debt To The Negro (continued)

Timothy, much to his discomfort. I would like to say here that she was the only white girl, in my eighteen years of teaching, I ever saw show anything but a disinterested friendliness toward a Negro boy. I heard of her actions from other teachers, but it had slipped my mind until one day Timothy's Latin teacher came to me in distress. She said Timothy had sobbed all through her class, and she could not get him to explain what was wrong.

After school, I sent for Timothy. He wanted to talk, and between sobs, I managed to piece out the story. It seemed that Jane had been making friendly overtures, like passing notes and wanting to walk from one class room to another with him, and Timothy had most persistently given her the "brush off". Her vanity hurt, and not being used to such treatment, she had written him a note that day, which he showed me, accusing him of thinking he was better than she. And then Timothy sobbed out, "Why, Mrs. Smith, I think the world of Jane, but if I walk with her or pay her any attention, people will talk about her. No nice white girl ever goes with a Negro boy." That, if you please, from that "dreaded race" that some people fear will insist upon social mingling of whites and blacks.

The third time I saw Timothy lose his self control was during his commencement week. All through senior high school he had returned to pay occasional visits, so I had been able to keep in touch with him. He had made quite a name for himself in the oratorical field, carrying off many state honors, and he always flattered me by coming back to rehearse his speech to me. At first, I had been able to help him, but by this time, he had far out distanced me in the fine art of speech making, and I think Timothy knew this as well as I. Nevertheless, it pleased me that he came back for my criticisms. He was graduating, now, with high honors and had won a scholarship. He had come back to me for advice.

Sitting there at a desk much too small for him now, he again sobbed out his troubles as he had done three years before: "I'm graduating, now, Mrs. Smith, and I've won this scholarship, but what can I choose for a life work? I could be a lawyer, but I'd have to just try the cases of my own race which would mean starvation for they are so poor, or else be a cheap shyster lawyer, and I won't be that. If I train to

America's Debt To The Negro (continued)

be a doctor, I can only doctor my own people, and though I'd like to serve them, and they need me, I must make a living. If I become a minister, the same would be true. If I train for a teacher, there are only a few colored schools open to me, and there would be no demand for my services. What must I do?"

Never in all my life have I felt so helpless. Finally, I laid my hand on his shoulder, and I think a Higher Power supplied the words, "Timothy, I can't tell you where you are going, but you must keep on. Use that scholarship and go to college. God didn't give you that fine mind, eloquent voice, and beautiful figure for nothing. He has a place for you and you will find it."

Timothy is now a trusted member of the Intelligence Service in Washington, D.C., and on his way up. I'm proud I had a chance to help give him his start.

All of my Negro boys and girls were not of Timothy's type. Like white children, they ranged all up and down the scale, from the very good to the very bad, from the highly intelligent to the lowest of the mentally handicapped, from the most diligent to the laziest human beings on earth, from the strictly honest to the lowest thieves one could imagine. But, always, I found them to have the same weaknesses and the same strong points as white children. I did find one difference. Because the Negro has so recently emerged from slavery, any of them have a much thinner veneer of civilization than the majority of white children. I read somewhere that it takes three generations to develop a lady or gentleman. The Negro child started with a handicap. If he were fortunate enough to have Timothy's background, he is off to a good start. But if he were like my Rosie, he is licked in the very beginning.

Rosie was in a group of handicapped children I had one year. They were styled by the office, "The Opportunity Group". That name puzzled me for awhile, and then I decided it meant there was opportunity to teach them anything and everything you could. They knew nothing to begin with.

Rosie's mother had three sets of children by three different fathers, though she had never been married to any of them, I had worked with her children from the other two sets and they were

America's Debt To The Negro (continued)

brighter than the average. Rosie's father must have been a dumb bell.

Rosie weighed over two hundred and she rolled down the corridors rather than walked. Each day when she came to class, she rolled up to my desk, gazed at me from her cow-like eyes, and asked the same question. "Miz Smith, kin I borrer a pencil?"

That pencil loaning worried me, because Rosie never used it to write with. She just lumbered to her seat, popped the borrowed pencil into her big, juicy mouth, and drooled and chewed all hour. Many were the lectures I gave, both personal and collective, to Rosie and the class, on putting pencils in your mouth. Rosie never heard them. At last I solved the problem by keeping a little box of pencils for Rosie's daily chewing. I don't know what happened to them. She never returned any, maybe she ate them up.

Once a term these groups had a free unit when we tried to encourage them to like books. It was difficult to find books simple enough for any of them to read. With Rosie it was impossible, as she couldn't read at all. In desperation, I handed her a picture book on Africa. Next day, her mother came to school in her best clothes and ire in her eye to find out why I thought her daughter would be interested in looking at a book on Africa. She was larger than Rosie, if anything. I'm afraid my answer wasn't very logical.

I liked my Negro children in the classroom. I found them, as a whole, friendly, eager to learn, and most appreciative of any kindness shown them. In the corridors, though, they were a problem. Usually there were never more than three or four of them in one class, and they probably didn't like the feeling of being outnumbered by another race. We wouldn't like it either. So they made up for it before and after school and lunch hours, by congregating in groups. There were nearly a hundred of them in the building. When they were assembled it not only was very noisy, but nearly always ended in a riot. The girls, especially, were prone to have hair pulling free for alls and scratch each other up as part of the day's work. For these reasons, teachers tried to break up all such gatherings, and by so doing, usually earned the ill will of many of them. In front of my door, which was at the foot of the stairway, was one of their favorite hanging out places. One of my most distasteful duties was scattering these groups.

America's Debt To The Negro (continued)

One day, I conceived the idea of a Negro club which would give them a place to meet together under supervision. The office gave me permission to try it and soon The Forum was in full swing. Nearly fifty boys and girls turned out to the first meeting, and we elected officers and mapped out a program. We decided to meet for one hour each week. The first twenty minutes would be given over to business and devotional matters. Then we would adjourn to the music room, where there was a victrola, and if they cared to dance they might.

Did they care to dance? Did they care to do anything else but dance? The answer was "No". Never have I seen such dancing. Never has anyone unless they have seen a Negro group in action. That room full of people was like one person swaying to the music. I've found myself swaying with them, completely carried away by the strange, savage rhythm of it all. Dancing to them is a religion as well as recreation.

Our club had many enjoyable meetings until Negro History Week rolled around. The school activity director thought, and so did I, that it would be a fine idea to have my Negro club give a program over the school broad casting system. The music teacher's help was enlisted and the program was a great success. A group from the club sang Negro spirituals and four of them gave talks on great leaders of their race. I found out, but too late to cancel it, that the program was arousing bitterness among the Negroes of the school. They didn't want to be singled out and get talked about in front of the whole school. They were Americans not just Negroes.

The next time my club met, only three or four loyal members showed up. The others might have drifted back, but while they were making up their minds, I disbanded the club. I believe it accomplished some good, but I was afraid to carry it on for fear it might do harm.

The Negro is unfathomable. He is working out his own salvation and doing it most successfully. He does not need social workers and reformers and uplifters. His own race can supply adequate numbers of highly trained, moral, cultured leaders for such work, who understand their people better than we do. What he does need from us is what the Constitution gives every American and that includes the Negro—the right to a free education, a free participation in the government, and a

America's Debt To The Negro (continued)

chance to earn a decent living wage. Let us see to it that he gets these things. Then the Negro problem will solve itself.

A True Experience On The Home Front

I was standing at the entrance of a low building waiting for someone. Two things I recall clearly. First, there was darkness, deep, inpenetrable darkness, on every side, closing me in and smothering me. Second, I had come a long way, and was still panting from the exertion.

Then the door opened, and a tall, young soldier with a rifle in his hand stepped out. The dim light of the room fell for a moment on his white gleaming teeth and dark eyes as he spoke to someone within. Then he pulled the door together behind him.

It was Jimmie, but I must have known all along that it would be he. I was not in the least surprised. Oddly enough, he gave no sign of recognition, but stopped to pull the bolt on his rifle to check the loading. Then he strode away into the darkness. I hastened to follow, not willingly at all, but vexed that I had to tramp around in the darkness when I was already dead tired.

I was fond of Jimmie. He had come in and out of my home, eaten at my table, shoveled my walks, washed my windows, made a fourth at bridge, many times, since I had moved next door to his parents. But I couldn't for the life of me see why I had to go with him now. Nevertheless, something impelled me.

Unable to keep up with his long strides. (Jimmie is six feet tall), I timidly grasped him by the arm expecting to be brushed off, as he was holding his rifle in both hands, but he seemed unconscious of me.

The going was bad. The ground was rough and uneven, through dense thickets and heavy vines that pulled at my feet. The high heeled mules I wore kept coming off and I was constantly stumbling against trees and into holes. At last I felt I could go no further. But, just at that instant before I could sink to the ground, something happened. I felt Jimmie's weight sink downward. I knew he was hurt. Forgetting, for the moment, my own exhaustion, I somehow pulled him up, and leaning on me, he turned around. Again we started that long trip back. At first he guided the way, conscious of me now, trying to walk, realizing his weight was too much for me. But, soon, he sagged downward again. This time I tried to pull him to his feet, he could not help, and I knew he was unconscious. I tried to lift him, but lacking the strength, I started dragging him by his feet, falling over limbs of trees,

A True Experience (continued)

into holes, gasping for breath, knowing I could never make it.

I called Jimmie's mother next morning to ask the latest news. No letter had come in several days. Mail from Guadacanal came through slowly in November, 1942.

In a few days the telegram came. Jimmie had been wounded while on a scout mission. It was the same night I had gone with him.

Our Children

I have no sons of my own, but in every corner of the world today, boys of mine are fighting and dying for their country. I gained the right to claim them as mine in the twenty years I spent teaching in one of our largest industrial cities. Not by the amount of book learning I imparted to them do they measure their loyalty to me. If that were all they would feel little gratitude. Few of my teen aged pupils were thirsting for knowledge, but many of them yearned for guidance and understanding. Many were the tragic tales of misery and heartbreak, growing, for the most part, out of parents misunderstanding and neglect that were brokenly confided to me during those years. When school was out my visitors came, some from my classes, others I had had the term before who had found a confidence in me, many older boys and girls, through school, coming back to the only place they knew for help, none of them bad, but all puzzled, unhappy, and temporarily lost.

Back of them, I could vision their parents, the ones who should have heard their stories, or better still, in most cases, the ones who should have prevented the need of them. Hard working, honest people, many of them foreign, all eager for their children to be good citizens, all striving to give them the advantages they had lacked, but helpless because they did not understand.

The sixteen year old girl who was not allowed to date or even leave the house in the evening because an older sister had gone wrong, and in desperation had run away to an aunt. The high spirited foreign boy whose parents kept him on bread and water, locked in their basement for a week, because he was a truant; the twenty year old German lad whose father had ejected him from the home in midwinter because he could find no job, and when he came to me, was sleeping in the park; the nineteen year old Catholic girl who went with a Protestant youth, only to find on returning, her clothes on the front porch and the door locked in her face.

These are only a few examples. There is not space to tell of more. And I was not an unusual teacher. When you work with human beings, you become interested in their welfare. All teachers who attain any amount of success establish personal contacts with their students. Even the foreman in the factories become interested in their workers

Our Children (continued)

and are concerned over any domestic or financial trouble that impairs their work. The student who is inattentive and wears a cloud upon his brow, challenges the teacher. "What's wrong, John?" is the natural question. If John's soul is burdened to the extent he must tell someone, he returns after school, and a way is often opened to help him over the hard place.

Someone inquires, "Why not tell him to go to his parents?" I ask you if a drowning man calls to you for help, do you suggest he find someone else?

The parents had failed him, had bungled their job. They have had no training in the serious business of rearing children and, lacking a miracle, their child will be a delinquent. In this national struggle to overcome juvenile delinquency why doesn't someone forget the child for a moment and give the parent a hand? Oh, I realize the Parent Teacher's Organization and others like it are trying to do this, but the surest sign of their failure is the growing number of Juvenile Delinquents in our country.

In the meantime, we need more teachers instead of less with the emphasis, not upon book learning, but character training and guidance. Home calls and visiting teachers to establish contacts with the home are being tried in some localities and proving most successful. Evening classes for parents of problem children should be established and in some way made compulsory. Instead of putting the boy on probation and making him stay in nights, we might try those things on the parent. Rearing children is the most important business in our country. Could we not spend a little time and money in training the people who do it?

War Brides

Thousands of words of consolation (and she deserves them all) have been penned in the past two years for the Mothers of service men. Paragraph upon paragraph, pro and con, have been written for and about the war besides. The children of war brides, also, have come in for their share, but so far I've found no word of sympathy for the war bride's Mother. There have been a few veiled illusions, it's true, to the parents of gold digging daughters who seemingly encouraged their off spring to descend upon some defenseless boy, tear him away from his loving parents, drag him before a minister, marry him out of hand, and attach his insurance and benefit checks. Most of these were written by old maids and didn't influence me much.

Now I take up my pen in behalf of the war bride's Mother. There must be many of them in this United States who feel as I do.

Two years ago, I was the proud Mother of two beautiful daughters, still in their teens, one working at her first position, the other in her last term in high school. Necessity having forced me to rear them alone, the path had been a difficult one. Delicate in health the load of keeping up my job, running the home, and being both mother and father to two lively youngsters had been a strain. Somehow, though, I had managed to do it, and in the fall of 1942 I felt I could relax and view my handiwork. Two finer, more dutiful and prettier daughters could not have been found. I was making plans for the younger one's college career, and it looked as if the hard part of my task was over.

Then came the deluge. Within two months both of my daughters were married, neither with my approval, and one without my knowledge. Both of the boys were fine, clean young men that I have come to love as my own chldren but at that time it was hard to take. That, though, was but the beginning. Do you feel any Mother enjoys seeing her young and sheltered daughter go chasing about the country from one military camp to another, living in small, poorly ventilated rooms, traveling on crowded trains, eating what and where they can, lonely and frightened and uncared for, often following some thoughtless boy, who even if he understood could be of little comfort; as he is not his own master? Now if those daughters are pregnant, and mine both were, the situation is still more complicated.

War Brides (continued)

Today I am a proud grandmother, my daughters and I are closer than ever, and I have two devoted sons-in-law. I have done what I could to pick up the pieces and help my youngsters. I don't feel too sorry for the boys. They are proud fathers, devoted husbands, and fine young men. Their responsibilities have acted as a steadying influence in their lives, and as they say, gave them something to work for. I can't see how the marriages have added to the anxiety of the boys' parents. It seems to me if I had a son in camp, I'd worry less about him if his wife were near, or if he spent his evenings writing to her. But I may be prejudiced here.

I do not feel too sorry for the daughters. It's true they grew up over night and gave up the light hearted, care free, girlhood, but, now they are having the time of their lives. Like the pioneer women of old. They are facing danger and standing shoulder to shoulder with their young husbands' glorying in their courage. We don't need to worry about them. The future of America is safe in the hands of such people.

But I do drop a tear in sympathy for the war bride's Mother, the unsung casualty of the Home Front, waiting and watching and wondering, at home, even though there is no service flag in her window.

Life From An Armchair

Two years ago at this time I was a professional woman, teaching in a large industrial city, and the sole support of two young daughters, one in her second year at college, the other ready to graduate from high school. Every moment of my day was full; there was not enough waking hours; I raced from one task to another, tireless, efficient, and happy.

Today I have plenty of time, more time than anything else. I sit in my arm chair or lie on my lounge most of the day, doing my best to get adjusted to the new way of things. For now, you see, I am a heart patient, and no longer run my own movements. I do what my heart wills, and he is often a stern disciplinarian. His punishment can be severe if I dare to disobey his orders.

But, at that, life is very pleasant. God has been good to me and left me many comforts. I still have my eyes. I can read, and write, and sew. If I grow tired of these I can just sit by the window and view the beautiful out of doors. I can still visit with my friends if I do it in moderation. I can listen to the radio and a thousand other things. I need no sympathy. Perhaps my affliction has given me the time to enjoy life.

The worst cross, at first, was the worry over my daughters. They had married, and when their babies came, I wanted to be beside them. In the beginning I fought against my helplessness – and then because I was so helpless and had to turn to someone for aid, I rediscovered a blessing I had almost forgotten in the busy years. I could pray about it. I learned again, to really "take it to the Lord in prayer". What a comfort it was. I just left everything up to God and then I closed my eyes and went to sleep.

My affliction has taken some things, but it has also given me much.

Life from an arm chair can be pleasant. My faith was rewarded a thousand fold and once more I was reminded of the futility of human beings without Divine Aid.

Eleanor Roosevelt

My American sense of good sportsmanship rises up to defend a fellow sister, a woman respected and loved all over the world, but one whose name is now being batted around by every crooked politician and cheap comedian at home, Eleanor Roosevelt.

Somebody, running out of missiles to cast at our President, threw the first stone, and it was something new for the bullies. Being a well-bred, dignified lady, she could hardly talk back. And, so, it has kept on, until you cannot turn the dial of your radio without hearing another cheap pun at her expense.

I have never met Mrs. Roosevelt, personally, but I love her wholeheartedly for her defense of the weak, her sense of fair play, and her broadminded straight forwardness. I'm not alone in my admiration, either. The service men down in the South Pacific will defend her staunchly. And so will many others.

I read in the paper where a man in England was arrested and fined because he made the remark that he liked the former Prince of Wales better than he did the present King and Queen. That happened in a country that is supposed to have a more democratic government than we do. Perhaps that story could prove that they do have. It certainly is no proof of freedom to allow unprincipled characters in our nation to slander the President and his wife.

Now, let us examine the charges brought against her. She travels. She even takes long trips without asking the American public and explaining to them her motive. She travels light we hear, so surely they don't suspect her of carrying soldiers' ballots.

Do we live in a land so despotic that the wife of our President must stay shut away from the public eye?

A Hobby Sneaks Up On Us

I've heard people remark about someone who had nice roses or plants, "She just has a gift for making things grow." Now, me, if I "merely look at a flower, it ups and dies."

From observations like these, I formed the idea, (if I thought about it at all), that flower lovers were born not made. I've since found out that that is just as much nonsense as the wide spread belief that some women are gifted with the ability of being good cooks. Anyone who can read, and is not lazy, can gain a reputation for cooking. The same is true of raising flowers.

My husband and I knew very little about flowers outside of the florist variety. We admired them in other people's yards, and were most appreciative when a friend occasionally gave us a bouquet. It is true that every spring we invariably spaded up beds and bought seeds and sowed annuals. But we were both employed, and after putting them in the ground we straightway forgot them. Unwatered and unweeded, the results were rather meager. Usually our efforts were rewarded with one or two stray nasturtiums and occasionally a few zinnias; nothing at all to make passers by stop and gasp at their beauty.

But that was before we found the house. We had played with the idea of buying a home, and always discussed it every time we paid the rent. Between times we forgot about it. Then one day in June, I was walking home from the bus, when I saw a vacant house with a "For Sale" sign on it. It was square and substantial looking and the front lawn was well landscaped. It was on a shady street and the porch with rose ramblers on each side, looked most inviting to me, especially so right then as I was warm and tired. Looking closer, I caught a glimpse of a backyard enclosed in a high, white fence. I'm not sure what prompted me, in a hurry as always and laden down with packages as I was, but I hurried up the walk and around the house to the yard gate. The very first peep and I was lost. There were at least a hundred kind of roses in that yard, all in bloom, not to mention peonies, clematis, and honeysuckle. The unmowed grass was half hidden with fallen rose petals, and it all looked so neglected and unmothered that my maternal instincts were aroused. I wanted to clean up that yard.

One glance at the real estate sign to get the name of the

A Hobby Sneaks Up On You (continued)

company, and I rushed home to telephone. My husband was somewhat alarmed at my impulsiveness, but when he saw the place, his heart was also captured. The next day we bought the house, and the following day we moved. Those roses couldn't wait. They must have a caretaker at once.

The former owner, a great lover of flowers, had died the year before, and since then the place had been vacant. Flowers are like children; they must be trained in the way you would have them grow. For a year there had been no pruning, nor training, nor spraying, nor any of the many things that yards require, and the place looked it. There we were. We had a ready made flower garden, that even in its neglected state, looked like an enchanted fairy land, but it was crying out for care. Something had been eating the roses. We could tell that, but we had no idea what. At that time, names like aphids and beetles and leaf hoppers were just not in our vocabulary.

It was characteristic of me, being a teacher, to turn to books for help instead of the neighbors. I had brought up my children by books, and learned to cook from books, and taught school by books, and I guess I'm just naturally one of those people who quote, not what the book says, but what the best authorities say.

We haunted the library, we searched out our "Better Homes and Garden" which luckily I had hoarded for several years, and we began studying. I started a file, which by the way, has become the most valuable aid we have. We ordered "The Garden Encyclopedia". We consulted authorities and sent to the state and national governments for information on insecticides and diseases. Then we went to work.

At first, we intended to clean up that lovely yard so we could enjoy it. We had visions of the luxurious lawn furniture we would buy, of the garden parties we would have and the long, lazy hours we would loll out there just doing nothing.

Somehow, those dreams never materialized. First of all, we had spent our money on sprays and pruning tools and insecticides, and there was none left for elaborate furniture. We contented ourselves with a lawn bench and some second hand chairs repainted. Even these were seldom used. Never did we sit down on one of them, but what we were sure to spy a bush that needed spraying, or a vine that

A Hobby Sneaks Up On Us (continued)

needed tying up, or a hedge that needed pruning.

This sounds like work, I know. Of course it was, but it was the most fun we had ever had. It wasn't long before we had the fever bad. We had joined the throng of flower lovers and gardeners. Every spare moment was either spent in our yard, or reading up on some insect or disease, or pouring over flower catalogues. "The Wayside Gardens", especially, became almost like a Bible to us, and I'm afraid, a great deal more used. For one thing we didn't know the names of many specimens we had and that was most exasperating. Only some one who has been through a like experience knows the inner struggle between annoyance and gratitude that can assail one, at a dear friend casually calling one of your flowers by name when you had been trying to identify it for months.

Then there were so many beautiful shrubs and flowers and vines in the catalogues that we did not have, and we were anxious to buy. When we first acquired our yard, it seemed perfection. Surely it contained every flower a person would want. But the more we learned about flowers, the more we seemed to lack. We must have delphiniums to go with our regal lilies, an Oriental poppy with our peonies, more iris, and canterbury bells, there was no mock orange, nor forsythia; in fact we soon discovered that outside of roses, clematis, and peonies, we had very little. In those groups, too, we were not satisfied. For instance, there were hundreds of other roses we wanted. We were anxious, too, to put name plates on them. Having unknown flowers is like forgetting the names of friends. Their faces are familiar, but you are at a loss just what to call them. Especially, is this embarrassing when you wish to introduce them to someone else.

Now a problem arose that seemed well nigh unsurmountable. Our back yard was twenty-five by forty, and we were sooner or later going to run out of space. Carefully, my husband, who was a draftsman, drew a plan of the yard. Each shrub and flower we had was drawn in according to scale and we considered the remaining space. Before new things were bought, it was decided exactly where they were to be placed. A few specimens that were not desirable were removed.

After a few years of this, as was inevitable, our yard became

A Hobby Sneaks Up On You (continued)

almost a source of annoyance to us. We felt cramped and there was no way to spread out. Our garden had become a beautiful place, a show spot in the neighborhood, but we were not satisfied. We wanted room for our hobby.

The idea of selling, and buying a country place kept growing on us. The first time it occurred, we recoiled from it in horror. To part with our yard was impossible. Then we attacked the problem scientifically. What did we have there we couldn't grow somewhere else? Wouldn't it be fun to start from the beginning and landscape our own place? Anyhow, our hobby was a life work. Too, the Victory Era had arrived. We wanted room for fruit trees, berries, a hundred things. We had found ourselves in that small yard, but must it confine our desires forever? We soon agreed that we must sell. The opportunity arose to do so with profit, and we have bought a small farm. So far there have been no regrets. For one thing, we are too busy fixing up our new home and will be for sometime to come, to think of the past.

I'll always be glad I walked down that shady street that warm day in June and spied that vacant house. It opened up a new life for us, a richer, healthier, and more contented one than we had ever known.

The Country Can Be Peaceful and Quiet

*(an answer to "It's So Peaceful And Quiet" –by Betsie De Beer Smith
in November issue of "Better Homes And Gardens".)*

I have just finished reading my November copy of "Better Homes And Gardens", an article entitled "It's So Peaceful And Quiet" – written by a city dweller, a Mrs. Smith who found nothing but disillusion in her move to the country.

In this day of vital home shortages thousands of other young couples have made that same move, and I dare say many of them found Betsie Smith's article biased, distorted, and one sided. On behalf of these other couples and my husband and I (another pair of Smiths) I ask permission to give the other side of the picture.

Born and reared in large cities, just as these other Smiths, my husband and I also succumbed to the call of the country. We found a little white house in Northern Michigan on the outskirts of a small village. It, too, had a beautiful view and little else to recommend it to a casual passerby. But to our enthusiastic eyes it presented countless opportunities, and unlike the other Smiths we set about by much hard work and very little money to realize them.

Our house also had 1880 wall paper. For four dollars we repapered our living room in a soft blue paper doing the work ourselves though we had never tried papering before. We painted the woodwork white and I slip covered our shabby furniture in flowered chintz. The result looked like an After picture in "Better Homes And Gardens". The windows were not to our liking and the beautiful view could hardly be seen from the front one, but after a hard day's work we could always enjoy it from our little front porch. We haven't had much time to sit and look out of the window, anyhow, but the white ruffled curtains, I hung at them make the house look attractive.

Our kitchen was dingy and also cup–boardless, but we found white oilcloth paper for the walls and a few hours of carpenter work could overcome those obstacles. My husband also found time to put me up a shelf for my Fiesta dishes and built me a bookcase. I slip covered an old studio couch and ruffled my shelf to match. The result was so pleasing we never tire of our homey kitchen. We weren't so lucky as the other Smiths with their electric range and running water — or were we? We had inherited a wood range like my grandmother

The Country Can Be Peaceful (continued)

used to use and I wouldn't relinquish it for anything. I even learned to bake bread in our oven and I've never tasted such baked beans as that old fashioned range turns out. My kitchen is a pleasant place on cold mornings. As for the hot days, I have an electric plate that serves very nicely.

We had a pump and a good well of water, the best in the country we were told, but we, being city reared, longed for a bathroom and running water. My husband is not a plumber, but instruction books can be bought and he wasn't afraid of work. Within three months we had a three piece bath, a cabinet sink (built from the very good material that was in the old outside toilet) and even a hot water tank attached to our range. The whole cost was less than two-hundred dollars.

Then like the other Smiths, we too turned our thoughts to poultry. We had a fair chicken house and felt we should put it to use. But having heard of the blunders made by amateur poultry raisers, we wrote to our State agricultural college and also the United States Department of Agriculture for help. Later we subscribed to two poultry magazines. We bought day old chicks also and we are now in our third year of the poultry business. We have not become wealthy but we are doing well enough at it, that my husband in another year, expects to make it a full time job. We have specialized in layers, and have built up a good egg business, we trap nest our hens, keep careful records, and find the whole thing most interesting as well as profitable. Our chickens don't wear diapers either, Mrs. Betsie Smith, but the modern trend is a built up litter that stays in the hen house a year and then at the end of that time makes a marvelous garden fertilizer. It's really worth carrying out.

We have had discouragements and we have made mistakes, but you know the old saying, experience is the best teacher. We have worked harder these three past years than we ever did in our lives but we have been repaid a thousand fold, in better food, fresh air, good health and most of all the triumphant feeling (our pioneer ancestors had) of building a home with our own hands. We have made a small income from our strawberries and vastly enjoyed them on our table. We have raised beautiful heads of cauliflower, broccoli, brussels

The Country Can Be Peaceful (continued)

sprouts, and many other rare vegetables, and can boast of our success with them. We had a good teacher as the first month we moved here we subscribed to "Better Homes And Gardens".

This year our fruit trees will begin to bear that we put out ourselves. My own hobby is flowers and only those who have tried it, know the pleasure I've realized from growing poppies, delphinimuns, foxgloves, canturbury bells and many other perennials from seed.

Unlike the other Smiths, the beauty of our little home, inside and out, does impress callers. We have had many compliments on our improvements.

Most of all it makes us happy — but not too happy to make still other improvements. That's one of the joys of country life. Your work is never done and tomorrow always calls you to some new task, but isn't that what makes a full and satisfying life?

We love living in the country and we wouldn't exchange our four room cottage for any city mansion.

Besieged By Ants

Were you ever under siege, that is, on the receiving end of a tremendous, all-out offensive? I was, this summer, and I was neither in Europe nor the South Pacific at the time but living quietly in my isolated country home here in northern Michigan.

The attackers, though not Japs, were much like them in their tactics—the large black carpenter ant.

During the latter part of August, we had decided to build a cellar under our garage, and the excavating was being done. About two o'clock, one hot afternoon, I started to step out of my back door when I met the enemy face to face, millions of them, coming from all directions, large, black, nasty ants, some flying through the air, (these scared me most), other swarming up the pillars and walls of the porch and along the walk and steps. Everything was literally covered with these repulsive creatures, some with long transparent wings, but all of them determined to take possession of my home.

Weaponless and defenseless, like any woman, I first slammed the door in their faces and stood on the inside trembling, only to discover three or four of the pirates scampering across my kitchen floor. Something must be done. First, I grabbed the tea-kettle, full of boiling water, in one hand and the broom in the other. So armed, I went forth again. I doused the scalding water on the proch. Aha, that helped, but futile with so many. Then I remembered the crude oil and kerosene, used that morning to spray the chicken coop—nasty, oily, stinking stuff that I had ordered kept away from the house. But, now, I welcomed it in my desperation. Noticing with relief that the spray was still half full of it, I hastily went to work, spraying like mad in a dozen directions at once, screaming in terror and disgust, as they lit in my hair and on my face and arms. Laugh if you wish, but I couldn't help it. Of all things in the world I fear insects the most. I will calmly step over a snake without turning a hair; even a mouse can't phase me, but let a spider, ant, or moth approach and I'm an utter coward. Nothing could have compelled me to have handled this situation had there been a man around. I would have at once become the clinging female, waiting to be protected. But no man was there. It was a matter of life and death – and I kept on spraying and squealing, for all the world like a Sinatra fan.

Besieged By Ants (continued)

Then it seemed there were fewer of them — their attacks not quite so persistent. It must be I was making some head way. Hopefully, I redoubled my efforts. The air was saturated with the pungent odor, my nice clean porch was dripping with the dirty mess, but I gazed with approval on the havoc I had created, and sniffed the reeking atmosphere with joy. The enemy was retreating. Soon not an ant was to be seen.

Now, that I could relax, I remembered a Michigan State College bulletin I had sent for on house ants that contained an article on the carpenter ant. Looking it up, I found, "Every now and then ant colonies produce large numbers of winged forms. These are the young queens and males. They swarm from the old nest, usually in considerable numbers, and attract attention by their abundance. Most of them die without causing injury. Probably not one queen in five hundred succeeds in establishing a colony."

In the same bulletin I found that kerosene pyrethrum spray was recommended for killing ants, so by a miracle, I had evidently chosen the right remedy.

True Tales of Kentucky
by a Mountaineer's Daughter

CHAPTER 1 — INTRODUCTION

In these days of gas rationing, when our "A" cards scarcely take care of emergency driving and we are all finding a little more time for conversation, have you noticed how most people like to tell of some favorite trip they took in those far off pleasant thirties when practically everybody owned a new car full of gasoline and could get a vacation at least once a year? I guess I'm guilty of it anyhow, for my friends are beginning to tell me about it. They say when I get a dreamy look on my face and a smile hovering around my mouth they know what's coming next. I'm going to launch out on another of those tall tales of my trip through the Kentucky mountains. I know it was one of the most pleasant summers of my life and I never grow weary of thinking and talking about it.

The daughter of a Kentucky mountaineer who had migrated to Michigan before I was born, I had dreamed all my life of visiting that enchanted region where my ancestors had lived for several centuries and where I had understood my "kin" was as numerous as the stars in the heavens. Being one of a family of twelve, (a mountaineer would feel it necessary to apologize for one smaller), I realized when very young that the visit would need to be post-poned until I could earn the where-with-all for the journey. To give my dream "legs", I early planned to become a school teacher. The reasons for choosing this profession were many, foremost among them being a natural aptitude for learning and a thirst for books that could never be satisfied in the environment in which I was reared. My father, a scholarly Southern gentleman, who had himself been a teacher in his younger days, giving up that profession, I imagine, when he acquired a family too large to support on a teacher's salary, encouraged me in this choice. My sister and I, with the help that Father could give us and by doing all sorts of odd jobs, managed to get through college, and one of the happiest days of my life was when I held my diploma in my fingers. My childhood dream would soon be realized and I could take my trip. I began teaching in one of Michigan's large industrial cities, and my dream like most dreams, soon got sidetracked. It was not until the summer of 1933 that I was able to carry out my plans. School being

Kentucky (continued)

out, I loaded my two small daughters, my aged mother, who wanted to see her old home before she died, my eldest sister, who had made the trip before, her twenty year old son who was to help with the driving, and far more baggage than we needed, into my new Chevrolet and turned her nose southward.

Eating up the roads as was the custom way back there in the thirties, as evening drew near we were approaching Magoffin County, Kentucky, our destination. The beautiful, hard, smooth highway that encircled these hills was a never ceasing wonder to my mother and sister. They had left this state in the latter part of the nineteenth century, but even in that length of time, it seemed incredible that such improvements could have taken place. The automobile, of course, had been responsible for the change. Gone were the bridle paths that had led over the mountains, and in their places were some of the best roads of the nation. We marveled at the perseverance and hard back breaking labor it must have taken to literally hew these roads out of the mountain side, for that was what had been done.

A more quaint, picturesque, home-like country than this could not be found in America. As we gazed on the peaceful little huts nestling in the valleys, hugging close to the foot-hills, surrounded by corn and potato patches, and noted the little family groups assembled on the stoops, we wondered where the fierce, blood-thirsty mountaineers of the movie and comic strips could be hiding, I might say here that we failed to find them in our visit to Kentucky. I came home realizing one fact. The Northerner has about as an exaggerated picture of the mountaineer as he has of the Eskimo. The taciturn, heartless, leary-eyed backwoodsman with a doubled-barreled, handle-notched shot gun grasped in his hand, a cud of tobacco clutched in his jaw, a year's growth of whiskers on his face, and a still hidden behind the house does not exist except on the screen. Moonshine still flows in these mountains, of course, but I will speak of that later. I merely wish to state here that these people crave peace and will go to extremes to get it. Maybe that is one of the reasons that Kentucky ranks third in the nation in the number of men who have volunteered during this war to fight the enemy and secure a lasting peace. Not bad for hill-billies when you consider the scant population

Kentucky (continued)

of their state. If the average movie fan could attend a "frolic" or "light and set awhile" on a mountaineer's porch in the cool of the evening, he would never recognize the merry, fun-loving group for the stupid-looking Kentuckians depleted on the screen. One should not forget that the kindliest humorist and greatest philosopher of our nation came out of these Kentucky hills; honest Abe was the son of a back-woodsman and he only grew up true to form. I am not advocating that there are other presidents coming from these hills. I must regretfully own that the timber necessary to build the popular type of president in vogue today, could not spring from the Kentucky mountains. It takes a sophisticated, cosmopolitan climate like New York to grow that kind of a flower. But, although politicians thrive in her midst, New York breeds no philosophers. Nor does any other modern city. On a humble mountaineer's stoop, from the lips of an old Kentucky woman, with a pipe clenched between her teeth, I heard words of wisdom fall that were never learned from a book written by some bigoted college professor. She had learned them in the school of life. And then she had pondered over her knowledge and it had ripened with the years even as their famed home-brewed ale is advertised to have done. Much wisdom and good have come from those mountains, and will, I firmly believe, come again. The people there have little of what the world calls wealth, but they get time to think.

CHAPTER II — A Mountaineer Home

That first night in Kentucky we stayed at Cousin Warnie's. The last mile it seemed to me we were traveling by submarine. They called it "fording the crick", but it is a most horrible experience. You see it was after dark when we were directed by an old woman to take the road leading up Middle Fork. I do not believe it ever gets as dark in Michigan as it does in the Kentucky hills. Anyhow, we were a long, long way from home in a strange country, and on a strange road. I suppose one could call it a road, but it led over hills and around precipices and through creek beds. We had long since left the main highway and were venturing far into what the children called the "sticks". It was pitch dark, and the lunges of the car as it crept over the

Kentucky (continued)

bumps reminded one of a blind man feeling with his stick. We had traveled since two o'clock that morning with only a light lunch, eaten from a paper bag, and we were both hungry and tired. For awhile we had talked and even joked feebly to keep up our courage, but that had ceased. I can't speak for the whole party, of course, but I'm not ashamed to own that I was homesick. I would have given almost anything to have been in my own house at home, rested and fed, and preparing to tuck my little daughters in for the night. They were, if possible, more weary than the rest of us, for their little weights had been shifted about frequently to ease the older members of the party.

The old woman had told us that we would have to "ford a crick" to reach Warnie's, and I felt a little like Christian must have felt when he approached the Slough of Despondency. I dreaded the future even more than the discomforts of the present and all I could do was to pray silently and fervently. At last we heard a splashing of water against the fender and knew that dreaded "crick" was reached. It could not have been more than six feet wide, but by the faint light of the moon, it seemed as broad as the Mississippi, and the girls cried out in alarm that we would be drowned. I was much of the same opinion, but did my best to comfort them. Mercifully the dreaded experience was soon over and at last we were across.

Peering into the darkness we could just make out the dim outlines of a house and other buildings enclosed in a picket fence. As Ralph started to unlatch the gate, three or four hound dogs from within set up a frightful howling. After five hundred miles of continuous traveling, even that sign of habitation was welcome to our ears. Then we breathed a sigh of relief, for we saw a faint light glimmer within. Almost instantly a voice called cautiously from the doorway, "Who's thar?" These mountaineers are the most suspicious people I have ever seen. They always open their door if they expect trouble, and in my brief stay among them I learned to instinctively dread seeing that door swing open. I always had the feeling that when it did I would be gazing into the barrel of one of their ugly looking guns. I decided this caution must be an out-growth of family feuds or maybe the dread of the "revenooers". Possibly my northern knock for admission had something to do with it. Kentuckians, much to my

Kentucky (continued)

horror, just open the door of a neighbor's house and go in without any kind of warning.

But, anyhow, we were all glad to see this door open. As I pulled my cramped limbs out of that crowded car, I was sure I could not have ridden another mile. Mother, old as she was, seemed to have stood the trip better than any of us. She was like a child on Christmas Eve, her eyes alight with anticipation.

It took some moments to explain just who we were, but with true Southern hospitality, we were asked to "light and set". Warnie remembered his Aunt Elizabeth and Ida, having gone to school with the latter. The rest of us he had never seen, but we were just as welcome for all that. As his quiet little woman routed her children (nine of them) out of bed and began to prepare a place for us, he plied us with eager questions about our journey. Scarcely could he believe that we had made the whole trip in less than fourteen hours. I was content for once to let some one else do the talking. After sizing up this first mountaineer rather hastily and noting him to be clean shaven, soft-spoken, gentle in manner, and very neat, I gave all my attention to helping fix the beds, offering, I fear, a very feeble protest against them putting their off-spring on the floor. The bed in the "front" room was assigned to me and my two little daughters. Most parlors in mountaineer homes boast of a bed with a beautiful counterpane and an immense feather bed as the chief piece of furniture. It didn't take the three of us very long to peel off our clothes and crawl between those snowy white sheets. As I sank deep into those downy feathers, I could only think how restful they felt to my weary limbs. The next moment I was sound asleep.

I was awakened next morning by the clatter of dishes in the adjoining room. With a feeling of luxury, I lay there for awhile, analyzing the tantalizing aroma that had reached my nostrils. Surely it did not lie. It must be that I smelled fried chicken, corn bread, and coffee. At least my mother had not exaggerated about the bill of fare when she had warned us that they would feed us chicken even for breakfast. Well, I wouldn't mind. With such a feast awaiting me, I could well afford to lie lazily in bed and take inventory of my surroundings. The house was divided into four rooms. I say divided, for there were no doors and I could lie on my bed in the corner and view the other three rooms. Two of these contained two beds each. These, with a couple of "stool cheers" and a bureau apiece, completed their furnishings. There were no rugs on the floors and no curtains at the windows, but every thing was spotlessly clean and gave signs of frequent scrubbings. The third room, from which the clattering came, must be the kitchen and dining room combined. Afterwards, I found out I was mistaken about this, and that there was a small lean-to beyond which served as the kitchen. No mountaineer, I discovered, ever eats in his kitchen. Such a procedure would be much beneath his dignity. The room I was lying in, gave certain signs of being the parlor, foremost among these being several enlarged portraits of prim, severe looking women and hairy faced men. Most of them, no doubt, my ancestors. The room, also, contained a mantel. The floor was bare and made of wide, rough boards. They must be what I had so often heard my mother refer to disdainfully, as "puncheon boards", a name that had held little meaning to me before.

By this time the girls had awakened. I had been wondering how we were going to be able to dress in a room totally lacking in privacy, but as the coast looked clear, we proceeded to try it. Soon we had joined the rest of the family already assembled in the dining room. Never had a meal tasted better nor been interspersed with more interesting conversation, for our host turned out to be a witty talker. He was the only member of the family who sat at the table with us, his wife and oldest daughter, a beautiful, dark-eyed little girl of sixteen, waited table, and the children, in order to show proper respect for us, waited.

This attitude toward children now seems to me to be the greatest difference between their homes and ours. Their children are kept in the background. They are literally seen and not heard. Many times they are not even seen, and in not one mountaineer's home were the children's accomplishments paraded before the guests. When they did appear they showed a deference to people older than they which could well be an example to us with all our boasts of culture and advancement. As a public school teacher, I have long deplored the manners, or rather lack of manners, displayed by the majority of children in our Northern schools. Not long ago, I sat in a group of teachers who were being addressed by the dean of a well known college, a good man and a wise man, who had taught the boys and girls of our state for many years. He told us that the outstanding characteristic of the students who entered his school was their lack of respect for authority and their discourtesy. I believe he wished to imply that the high schools were not training their pupils in these qualities, and he, no doubt, was right. But, here in these mountaineer homes where school lasts about six months out of the year, and at its best is a rather poor makeshift of an education, these children are courteous and well-behaved. There seems to be no severe punishment, either, nor any need of it. These children are fed and clothed, rather negligently I fear, and then forgotten. Maybe, therein lies the secret. As both parent and teacher, it has always been a pet theory of mine that half the dismeanors of children are to draw the attention of their elders, and here that theory seems to be proved. They had learned, evidently, that nothing short of a broken limb would win them any notice, and they had given up trying.

Although they may be getting better training in a certain kind of courtesy than our own children, I somehow wouldn't want ours patterned after them. There was something pitiful about these little mountaineers that went to my heart. They reminded one for all the world of a little stray puppy with no one to love and pet it, and they are just as grateful for attention as that stray puppy would be. Now I'm not saying that mountaineers do not love their children. There are all kinds of proofs to the contrary. But mountaineers are a very reserved people. They seldom give any demonstrations of their feelings. Perhaps these little children are unable to peer through the shell that encases their parents' love and discover the beautiful contents. Anyhow, I am glad I do not live in a community where a child's good-night kiss is unknown and its little voice silenced in the presence of its parents. With a total lack of toys and books, one wonders what they do to pass the time away. I know my own two daughters were glad to start for home when the time came.

After breakfast, Warnie had to go to work, (an F.E.R.A. project, I believe,), but, as we wished to call on other relatives and needed a

Kentucky (continued)

guide, his eldest son was instructed to do the honors. When I was presented to this young man, I was rather surprised to find he was a college graduate and had taught school one year. He was as poised and well-dressed as any University man and Kenneth (for that was his name), and I were soon talking shop just like any two teachers do when they get together.

Leaving our baggage at Warnie's, and with Kenneth acting as guide, we "forded the crick" again and proceeded up Bare Branch toward Salyersville. As we drove along, Ralph began telling Kenneth how worried I had been the day before over our money. Some weeks before we had started on our trip, we had read about a young couple from our own city, who had been traveling through Oklahoma, when they were attacked by robbers, who took all their money and possessions, even their car, and left them on foot. As I thought of this story and as the country became more wild and uninhabited at every mile, I decided to take precautions. Stopping the car at a gas station, I went to the rest room and hid a twenty dollar bill in my stocking, so in case were were held up we might escape with that.

Just at that point in Ralph's story, I ceased to listen. I had more important matters to attend to. Hastily, I peeled off my stocking, but alas, my worst fears were realized. No money was to be found, and I gave one agonized howl. Remembering I had sat on the side of that glorious bed the night before, and taken off my shoes in the dark, I could only hope the bill had fallen to the floor, and might yet be lying there. The family was aghast at my carelessness, for, to a teacher, the loss of a twenty dollar bill was then, as now, a very serious matter. It didn't take long to turn the car around and drive back to Warnie's. And then that terrific search began. Starting with laughter and self-assurance, it dragged on until we were all in the midst of despair and ill-temper. The bill was not on the floor by the bed nor was it on any other floor. That little wife had made her beds by this time, perfect works of art, each feather tick beaten and smoothed until no one could have found a lump, (above all other accomplishments Kentucky women pride themselves on their bed making and a woman who cannot make a bed that meets with their approval is absolutely no 'count).

Kentucky (continued)

Nevertheless, that bed as well as all the other four, was torn apart. Suitcases were emptied, bureaus searched, closets turned out, but all to no avail. The little woman insisted on searching every nook and cranny in her home, but the money did not come to light. Not only was I growing desperate, (for that bill was half of our expense money), but I saw black looks on the faces of my loved ones. I saw, too, and my heart grew heavy at the sight, that these dear people under whose roof we were, thought I suspected them of stealing it. Such a thought I had never entertained for one moment, but how could I prove my faith to them? Certainly not by abandoning the search. That must go on. Then my sister, the traitor, gave up in disgust, and even said she thought I had left it in the rest room instead of putting it into my stocking. Sick with discouragement, humiliated, and now alone, I refused to give up. In despair, I called Ralph and Kenneth into a conference. Pleading with them to stand by and assuring them I knew no one had taken it, we tried to conquer the situation by thought. At last Ralph suggested that we search our shoes.

It seemed a silly idea, but it was something to do. The grown people finished theirs and we called to the children. Barbara took off hers and we began on Marjie's. Her first one proved fruitless, and I turned away. I had given up. We would stay forever in those hills, or else they could loan us the money to return home. (After this stunt of mine they would probably give it to us if we would leave). Down through the years my relatives would tease me about that lost bill. Life was bitter — and then a shout from Ralph as he held Marjie's other shoe in his hand. There, reposing quietly through all the trouble, the bill lay where I had dropped it the night before when I had taken off my stocking.

How relieved we all were, but that did not end my shame. I know I shall never think of those kind people without remembering how I upheaved their household that morning, and I am sure they will always think of me as that crazy Northern woman who carried her money in her shoe.

CHAPTER III — Aunt Het

Up on Bare Branch we found Aunt Het and her large family settled

Kentucky (continued)

round her. There we decided to yield to their urgent persuadings and "stop a spell". Aunt Het was the widow of my mother's brother. He had died some years before, a prosperous man by mountaineer standards, and due, no doubt, to Aunt Het's influence, had left a most peculiar will. The house and grounds were willed to his widow, but the large estate was to be evenly divided among his twelve children, providing they would when becoming of age, build a house on their portion and live there. Otherwise, their part would revert to their mother. So here they all lived, their little huts encircling their mother's larger home, for all the world like an old Virginian plantation, with its outlay of Negro cabins. And the comparison did not stop here. Aunt Het was the manager of the plantation and the Negro driver. Although she carried no black snake whip, there was not a human being, young or old, on that whole Bare Branch, who did not leap to do Maw's bidding, for that was what they called her, when she spoke.

As I looked at that old crone, I wondered wherein lay her power. Aged, and shriveled, and bent, she could not have weighed seventy pounds. Her black hair, (still black despite her seventy-four years), was parted in the center above a low forehead, and done in a smooth knot at the nape of her neck. Beneath projecting eyebrows, peered out two gleaming eyes. Her nose was long and hooked. Her face was small and thin and wrinkled and as dark as an Indian's, with high-cheeked bones. Between her thin lips was clenched a brier pipe, held in place by the only two teeth she possessed. Ralph very aptly styled her Mahatma Ghandi, and just as strong was her leadership in her small world as his in India. But, despite her domineering nature, there was a humorous twinkle lurking in those shrewd old eyes of hers. Recognizing a character, I set out to cultivate her, and before I left Kentucky, a strong attachment had sprung up between us. Historian, humorist, and philosopher, I found her, and for many of the stories I treasure, Aunt Het is responsible.

Bare Branch was scarcely accessible by car and after bumping over the worst road I was ever on and riding down a creek bed, it was small wonder that having arrived without mishap, we were content to remain in this hide-out for awhile before bumping back to civilization. We were welcomed most royally, and I sank down on that stoop

Kentucky (continued)

contentedly and returned not a word when one of my masculine cousins despatched a horse and rider for our baggage and informed us we were going no further.

I chose the first house for my headquarters because the car could not penetrate further up the Branch and I was too tired to walk. It had not yet occurred to me to ride horseback. Afterwards I found that house had other advantages. With the exception of Aunt Het's big house, it was the only one that had screens and an outhouse. It also boasted a pump, the only one for miles around. As I had been warned of the dreaded malaria lurking in Southern wells, I resolved to keep my family near that pump. In the day time, though, we all assembled at Aunt Het's for the never ending supply of fried chicken and hot breads, and beguiled the time away by eating and visiting.

CHAPER IV — Witchcraft

Aunt Het, Susie, (my cousin's wife), and I were sitting on the back stoop preparing string beans for dinner. I haven't mentioned Susie yet, but she had been there all the time. Very much there in fact. She was the kind of person who could not be overlooked, a regular mountain of a woman, slovenly, unkept, barefooted, and uncorseted; a typical mountaineer's wife. I had seen several of them in my brief visit in the hills. They all fitted one pattern, and from their appearance, I had been able to deduce the following: After a mountaineer girl marries, she must lose her vanity. No longer need she adorn herself with pretty clothes, nor arrange her hair becomingly. It is not even necessary to keep neat and clean, for has she not won her race? She has caught her husband, and now her duty is to stay at home and "fotch up her young-uns". At the very period when most Northern women concern themselves most about their clothes, their permanents, and their facials, the mountaineer's wife sits down, complacently, and lets Nature do her worst. In Susie's case, that worst had been tremendous. As I looked at her bulky, uncorseted figure, her dirty dress, and black, greasy hair stringing down around her coarse face, I wondered how my fastidious cousin was able to abide her. I had heard inklings of some of his philanderings and I could scarcely blame him. At least, I thought, she could keep clean. My mother had been a mountaineer, but I had never seen her dirty. When a tiny child, I had been taught that cleanliness was next to godliness.

Strange as it may seen, this slovenliness does not appear to be a trait of the mountaineer men. They are clean-shaven, neatly dressed, and carry themselves well. On horseback, in their neat riding clothes and broad-brimmed hats, they look very handsome. They appear young for their age, never having come in contact with hard work and knowing little of worry, which are the two thieves of youth in the North. They are athletic in build, a fat man being absolutley unknown among them.

It is true that mountaineer men seldom take their wives to town with them, but the only mode of traveling is by horseback and many of their women have given up riding because of excessive weight.

There were some mountaineer women who differed from Susie. Aunt Het for one, who had her own bay riding mare, and on her old fashioned side saddle, was often seen riding with one of her many sons. My great Aunt Mary was another. Although past eighty, she rode over eight miles to see us, alighted from her own horse, unassisted, and came swinging up the walk like a young girl. I shall tell more of her later. Cousin Kate, Aunt Het's baby girl, was another example. She was as trim and well groomed as any girl of my acquaintance. Her petite figure was always daintily arrayed, her naturally curly hair becomingly arranged, and her makeup skillfully applied. As alert in mind as she was pleasing in appearance, (and have you ever noticed that these two qualities usually go together?), she had ridden horseback twenty miles to a neighboring town for six years until she had a Teacher's Certificate, and now taught the local school. She was the best horsewomen in the country, the most graceful dancer, and the mainstay of her mother, with whom she made her home.

But as I said, we were fixing string beans for dinner when Susie's baby crawled out on the stoop. A beautiful child, but as unkempt as her mother and wearing but one garment—a dirty sack of a dress (in the mountains all small children go without any sign of diapers or pants, their little bottoms bare to the world), she at once became a target for the shrewd old eyes of Aunt Het.

"What ails that youngun, Susie? She looks right puny to me." "I

Kentucky (continued)

reckon she's done been ailin with trench mouth, Maw. I been fixin arter sendin Jim over on Lick Skillet to fetch the old witch to blow smoke in her mouth, but we just been puttin it off."

"Why, surely, you still don't believe in those old heathen customs down here," I exclaimed. "If she were my baby, I'd wash her mouth out with a solution of boric acid"—and then I stopped abruptly when I saw the sullen resentment of Susie's face at my interference. Aunt Het, too, shook her head emphatically.

"Now, honey, the trouble with you Northerners is, you're jest plain ignorant. Wish to my never see, if you ain't plum foolish when you say you don't believe in witches. Why, child, didn't you ever hear about the time your great grand pap, Lige Minnix, set out to learn how to be a witch?"

I confessed I never had, so Aunt Het launched into the following account of my great grandfather:

"Your great grand pap was a right smart man. I can jest shet my eyes and see him comin down the branch, now, carrying hisself jest as straight as a sapling, though he was nigh eighty year old when I rekellect him. But this story I'm going to tell you happened when he was a deal younger. You see, he uster to live over on Lickin River at that same place whar you went to see your Cousin Freeman, last night. Times wa'nt so good in them days. It were right arter he got home from the war, and his slaves was all gone and them pesky Yankees had took his hosses and cattle and 'bout ever' thing else of any 'count. Reckin they'd left him Mary and the younguns. Your Maw's told you 'bout your great grand Maw, Mary, I reckin. The hull family set a lot of stock by her. She uster be a midwife, and knowed right smart 'bout medicine. You favor her a heep, honey, with them blue eyes of yours and that high for'ed. Uster ride 'stride jest like a man. No decent women ever done that in them days. I reckin they talked right smart 'bout her, but they were plum glad tew see her comin when some of their young uns was ailin'. I've done heerd that with the war and all the men folks gone, times would have been a lot wusser if it hadn't been for Mary Minnix. That woman, I reckin, wasn't feered of nuthin'. Now, I reckillect it as how they uster say she didn't believe in witches, nuther. But I done sot out to tell you 'bout old Lige and lak I war a sayin', when

Kentucky (continued)

he come home from the wars, things was in right bad shape. Ther'd been high water and the tobaccer patch his young uns had planted was washed out. Everything had gone to rack and ruin. Right 'bout that time, as luck would have it, an old witch doctor come along. He told Lige thar was a bad spell throwed on him, and if he'ed get tew be a witch doctor hisself, he could break the charm. Mebbe, tew, if he'ed get to be a right good one, he could conjer up some better luck for hisself. Wal, your great grand pap knowed he couldn't make things no worser, so he kakalated as how he'ed try it. The old witch doctor said it would cost him fifty cents (that war a sight of money in them days), but they'd hafter go back in the hills apiece so no one would pester them. Lige jest waited long enough tew grab his six shooter and old black hat and he tuk arter that old witch doctor, lickety split.

Pears like he'ed jest had so much bad luck he didn't keer 'bout nothin'. When you get as old as I am, you'll find out that thar's nothin' like a war tew shake a man's faith in man and the Almighty, tew. Reckin as how he figured God had gone back on him, so he'ed try the devil. Spect, tew, he'ed been 'round right smart and had noticed as how the devil's very offen 'pear tew be the lucky ones. Jest 'pears tew be, I said, honey," as I started to protest, "The devil knows his own and claims them in the end."

"Wal, as I war tellin' you, Charley Cole, that war the old witch's name, led him back a right smart piece in the woods, and then he tuk him up a big hill. Then he told your grand pap if he would do p'int blank what he told him, from that day on he could have power over anything and everybody. Your grand pap war right smart pleased and went tew work with a will. Wal, the fust thing he had tew do war tew swear he would never tell a liven' soul what war goin' tew transpire. Then Old Charley 'splained he would have tew draw a ring 'round him and repeat arter him, this rhyme:

> All I have, I now Forsake
> And Satan to my heart I take.
> No other God but him ther'll be
> If he'll, now, but grant to me
> Power of magic and of charm
> That I may wreck my fill of harm.

Kentucky (continued)

From now on I am your servant,
If you will me this power grant.

"Your grand pap got that part done tolerable quick, and then Old Charley told him he must shoot at the sun seven times, each time cussin' God's name. At the seventh time, a black man would appear with a bloody handkerchief. This he would give tew your grand pap, and as long as he kept that handkerchief he could work any charm he wanted tew. Your grand pap war kinder shaky 'bout this. He had done been fotched up a Hard Shell Baptist, and it war a purty big thing for him tew cuss at God. But thar war no turnin' back now, so he raised his gun and fired at the sun. Jest as he started tew cuss, the sky got black as night an it started tew thunder and lightnin'. That war enough fer your grand pap. I reckin he thought the world war comin' tew an end fer sho'. Instead of cussin', he dropped his gun, fell on his knees, and begun tew pray."

"Old Charley war awful mad. He went so fur as tew threaten tew kill your grand pap, but it warn't no use. Lige jest picked up his gun and went home, and I reckin that war the only one of your kin I ever heerd tell on tryin' tew be a witch doctor."

- -

"Speaking of witches, Aunt Het, did you ever see a witch ball?"

"Wal, lordy mercy, honey, it's been so long, I'd plum nigh fergot, but 'pears as how I do rekillect seein' one, onect. It war when I war jest a mite of a child 'bout the size of your Barbary thar that I seed that one."

"Maw had sent me up on the hill arter the cows. I had gotten them all turned fer home 'ceptin' Flower. I can jest shet my eyes and see her yet. She war red and white pied and the purtiest critter you ever did see. She war my maw's favorite heifer and she done sot a lot of stock by her. Wal, this night I war speakin' 'bout, Flower acted right quar. When the other cows turned t'wards home, she stood still, and I jest coudn't git her tew budge, nohow. She jest put her head up and mooed and acted so peculiar like, that at last I run tew fetch Maw. Wal, it tuk Pap and Maw both tew git her down the hill, and then she went backwards with her tail fo'most, all the way. We tried tew git her tew drink water, but she wouldn't do one thing, but moo kinder mournful like, at the sun. Maw said she war bewitched, and she knowed who done it. So she sent Pap arter Old Charlie Cole, the witch doctor. As soon as he kum, he jest rubbed his hand sorter gentle over her back and said some quar rhyme, and wish to my never see, if that heifer didn't turn right around and walk into her stanchion by herself. But, afore she went in, she spit up a witch ball. Maw picked it up and kept it 'till she died; then I don't rekillect what become of it."

"However, Old Charlie Cole told Pap that it had three of Flower's hairs in it, mixed in some flour and other stuff. He said that afore you could bewitch any one, you had tew git somethin' that belonged tew them, 'course, with a cow, it would have tew be a hair But he told Pap how he could break the spell if he know'd who done it. Wal, Maw, she said twar old Sal Higgins, so Old Charley told Pap tew fill his gun with water and plug it up and set it in the chimney corner. Whoever had cast the spell on Flower would come tew borrer somethin', cuz they wouldn't be able tew pass water 'till the spell war broke. He told Pap tew be sure and not loan her nuthin'."

"Wal, honey, shore nuff, the very next mornin', afore sun-up, Old Sal Higgins kum and wanted tew borrer a chaw of tobaccer. Pap made some skuce that he war purt nigh out, and she went away agin. That night she kum back and wanted Maw tew let her have some coffee. Maw told her she didn't have none. Wal, honey, the next mornin', afore we war skeercely up, she kum arter the sheers. She told Pap if he wouldn't let her have them, she'ed die. I reckin he thought she'ed been punished enuff, so he axed Maw tew git them fur her. As Old Sal stepped in arter the sheers, jest as she got her hand on them, the water flew all over the room, jest p'int blank like a flood. Now, honey, she never put no more charm on Pap or Maw nor none of them from that day on, and I seed that with my own eyes."

CHAPTER V — A Mountaineer "Meetin' "

Going to church, or as they call it, "goin' to meetin' ", is a much more looked forward to event in the mountains than it is in the North. For one thing, they have no building for a place of worship, and either hold their meetings at the school house or out of doors. The latter place is much more popular in the summer months and was where I

Kentucky (continued)

attended.

Another reason that makes church seem a sort of treat to them is that they have traveling ministers that only reach their locality every seven or eight weeks. Between times, if they wish to hear a sermon, they can ride nine or ten miles on horse back to where the preacher is holding forth.

This can be most inconvenient — at certain times, especially if the occasion of a wedding or funeral arises. The way mountaineers got round the problem of the latter, I thought was interesting. It's much better when people die at the time the preacher is handy, but in case they don't, the relatives just have them buried and wait for the preacher to hold the funeral when he returns. This sounds quite simple but, many times, people die at too rapid a rate for one poor preacher to care for them all on his next visit. They sort of pile up on him, so to speak, although that is a gruesome way of putting it, and that is why that many times a person has been dead for over a year, before the funeral is preached.

Now, it so happened that such a funeral, and that of a close friend of Aunt Het's, was being held up on Breathitt, at the head of the Branch, and about eight miles away, the last Sunday of our visit. Aunt Het was determined we should not return North until we had heard one good "preachin' ", so it was decided that we should attend this meeting. As I had taken up horse back riding, more from neccessity than for pleasure, Aunt Het loaned me her old bay mare and side saddle for the occasion, and Kate and I rode those eight miles while Ralph took my sister, mother, Aunt Het, Susie, and Jim in the car.

Maybe some of my readers know how to dress for church and horse back riding at the same time. I didn't then, but I learned. Kate showed me how to neatly fold my silk dress up around my waist before I donned my slacks. When we reached our destination, off came our slacks, and presto–we were all dressed for church.

Maud, Aunt Het's old mare, was a stubborn and contankerous as her mistress, and evidently, as good a judge of human nature. She sensed at once that I was green, and no amount of urging would make her move out of her slow, pokey, old walk. Kate hung along beside me and tried to help, getting much amusement out of the way I addressed

Kentucky (continued)

my steed. Not being versed in Haw, Gee, and Giddap, I talked to her in true school teacher fashion, as I did to my pupils. Like my pupils, she paid very little attention, and I was growing desperate. Then Kate suggested that she trot on ahead and Maud would go faster to catch the other horse. It worked - only too well. I rode most of that eight miles in the air, always coming down at the wrong time. John Gilpin's famous ride was nothing on mine, and Aunt Het's old side saddle was not much help. But Maud went faster and faster, (she was truly a beautiful pacer), and I either had to learn to ride or break my neck. By the time we reached out destination, I had learned, the hard way, "to sit my saddle". After that it was easy, but for a few days I felt mighty uncomfortable. Not even Aunt Het's praise that I rode like a real Kentuckian, was salve to my wounds, (I mean that literally).

The car, of course, had left us far behind, so when we reached the appointed place, we were a little confused as we could see gatherings at the tops of two different hills and we weren't sure which group our relatives were attending. Tying our horses to a hitching post, we climbed up one mountain, which after my wild ride was quite an undertaking, only to be told that our kin was over on the other mountain. As an after thought, our informer added, "Thar's right smart drinkin' goin' on over thar."

Much more slowly we ascended the other hill and recognizing our friends, drew near the gathering.

Seats had beem built by setting planks into the side of the hill, forming sort of bleachers. Here the congregation sat. We slipped into a vacant place on the back row, and I noticed boxes of cake and bottles of liquor were being passed up and down the rows. The women took very dainty helpings, some refusing altogether, but the men partook liberally of both food and drink. I'm not sure, yet, but what it was their way of taking communion. If so, they all seemed to be enjoying it.

In front of the group was a sort of box like arrangement where the chief mourners sat, all of them weeping and wailing as if the object of their mourning had but died the day before. I wondered if, unless it was someone very dear to them, they found it hard to save up their tears over such a long period. Be as it may, they were doing very well. I was much surprised to see Aunt Het and my mother in their midst, the

Kentucky (continued)

latter weeping copiously as any of the other mourners, although I knew she had never seen the woman whose funeral was being held.

In the center of the mourners, but a little to the foreground, stood the preacher, a most picturesque figure, but resembling a Western cowboy far more than he did a man of God. He wore riding breeches, a wide sombereo, and a revolver on each hip, one hand, rather by accident, I suppose, resting on the handle of one.

I wish I could write down that sermon word for word, Maybe it's well that I cannot, because there may be many good ministers in those hills, well trained in the word of God and a credit to their profession, even if I did not meet them. I saw only this one queer impostor, and his sermon went something like this; punctuated by the fervent amens of the men of the congregation as they enthusiastically guzzled their liquor: "It says in the good book, amen, that Abraham went into the land of Canaan, amen, flowing with milk and honey, amen, brethren, we must follow the word of God, as He did it to the least among you so he will do it unto me"—and he continued on and on, all given in a kind of high sing-song voice for all the world like the ritual of a tribe of savages. At first I really tried to follow, because there is nothing I enjoy more than a good sermon, but I soon discovered it was all pretense; he was actually saying nothing, but a jumble of words, Nevertheless, if you could judge from the rapt, attentive faces of his audience, as far as they were concerned, he was quite all right. All at once, I had an insane desire to howl with laughter. While I was trying to choke back this impulse, I happened to catch Ralph's eye. He was, evidently, having the same difficulty, and it was just too much. We began to rock back and forth in a burst of side splitting laughter, expecting every minute, as we confided to each other later, to be the target of that preacher's six shooter. Nothing happened. Maybe he thought we were showing our approval, or maybe (as I strongly suspected), he was too drunk to notice.

Kate nudged me once during the sermon, to point out a meek, pious, little woman that she said had killed three husbands and was now living with a fourth one. They couldn't get any judge or jury to convict her as she was related to all of them. I privately made a mental note, if I ever had any crimes to execute, I'd return to Salyersville

Kentucky (continued)

because every man, women and child in the town claimed relationship with me. So far, I've not been back.

As we left the gathering, Aunt Het remarked to me, "Honey, when you git back tew Michigan, I reckin you kin tell them heathen Northerners you heerd one sermon that war the true word of God."

CHAPTER VI — "Mountaineer Frolics"

Kate had been teasing Jim to let her have a "frolic" at his house while we Northerners were there as Aunt Het was firm in her refusal to open her house to one. Cousin Jim was somewhat reluctant at first, because he was a Hard Shelled Baptist, and in their eyes, dancing was a sin. Jim was afraid he would be "churched" if he allowed such a snare of Satan to be perpetrated in his home. That word "churched" puzzled me at first, but I soon found it meant to be thrown out of the church, quite a common incident in those parts. To me, a religion seemed rather inconsistent that would condemn a man for dancing, but would ignore his drinking and could even condone a murder if it were in protection of his honor or his woman. At length, though, Jim was persuaded, and the date of the frolic was set.

The plans, or perhaps I should say, lack of plans, for the party were most interesting. Kate got on her horse and rode down to the school house, a common meeting place for the young people of the neighborhood. Here, she casually dropped a remark that there was going to be a frolic at Jim's on Wednesday night, and left it to the person who overheard her to spread the news. It would be very bad form, I gathered, to do your own inviting, something on the order of a social climber. I was rather skeptical of anyone coming on such a roundabout invitation as that and privately decided it was going to be "some party". As no effort at all was made to secure music for the dancing, that opinion strengthened, and I was feeling disappointed, for I had set my heart on that party.

Wednesday finally arrived and I got up early, prepared to help Susie and Kate take the house apart and clean it from garret to cellar as I always did at home when I expected company. Nothing of the sort happened to Susie's house. There was no extra cleaning, nor cooking, nor pressing of clothes, nor any other activity to mark this day as

Kentucky (continued)

different from any other. Now, I was sure they really didn't expect anyone and had just been humoring me. But, as evening approached, I grew a little nervous. Someone might come, I thought, and I for one wanted to be ready. I heated water for my and the girl's baths which we took every day in the smoke house, At first I had been hard put to it to find a place private enough to bathe in a doorless house, until Susie had suggested the smoke house. It had a door I could fasten, and it was very cool and clean, and the girls and I got a great deal of fun bathing in the presence of the hams. Where Susie bathed, I don't know, if she ever did.

I dressed the girls in their simple organdy dresses, the likes of which the mountaineers had never seen, judging from the excitement they caused, but no one else having cleaned up. I contented myself by putting on a fresh house dress and arranging my hair. Then I began to wonder where they would dance if they did come. The only room at all large enough, the parlor, had a bed in it that took up nearly half the floor space.

The first hint I had of anything really going to take place, was when Kate asked if I would drive her over to Salyersville to get the musicians. I couldn't get her there fast enough to suit me, and soon we were on our way home with a four piece orchestra, each and every one who claimed to be some rank of cousin to me, and all four of them as dapper young men as you could find around any Northern dance hall.

When we got back, the guests had begun to straggle in, mostly shy gawky girls and awkward, sheepish looking boys. A few older people came, too, not to dance, heaven forbid, but just to look on and size up the Northerners. All of them made excuses for dropping in like we might do at a surprise party, and when about forty had assembled, Kate asked Jim if he would let them dance. He reluctantly gave his consent, acting much surprised at the request, just as if he had never heard of it before, and two or three of the young men began taking down the bed. Then, and not before, Susie retired to a corner of the bedroom and changed her dress. The furniture was pulled back, the orchestra tuned up, the married folks formed a circle with their chairs around the room, the young men chose their partners and led them

Kentucky (continued)

into the circle and the frolic was on.

Never have I seen such dancing. It resembled the Northern square dance, but was much, much faster, and everyone sang to the music. Old-fashioned jingles, known for years in the mountains:

"Prettier than a red bird, prettier, too,

I can get another one, so can you,

Skip to my Lou, my darling,"

and similar ones. Ralph and I were soon a part of the whirling, merry group, and never have I had more fun.

Several of the young men, I found, had worked a winter or two in factories in Detroit, Michigan, but had been homesick, there, and drifted back home. In spite of their preference for the hills, I noticed they were more fashionably dressed than the others, their hair was slicked down, they had a more sophisticated manner, and showed a pathetic interest in what was going on outside. (By the way, in my entire visit in the mountains, I saw no newspapers, radios, or books). These same young men, now must, at least most of them, be in this war. If they fight as well as they played the violin and danced, they cannot help but make a great contribution for Uncle Sam.

CHAPTER VII — Beliefs and Superstitions of the Mountaineers

No where in America today could one find another group of people so credulous, dreamy, and superstitious as the Kentucky and Tennessee mountaineers. There are several reasons for this, foremost among them being the geographical formation of the mountains which close these people in from outside influences.

Early in our history, during the days of Daniel Boone, there was a strong Scotch-Irish influx in to these hills. There these Anglo-Saxons settled down and there they are today, their blood stream scarce touched by any other nationality except, occasionally, a strain of Indian, the people they conquered. There has been no migration from the outside, and the mountaineers marry among each other, unions between first or double cousins being a common procedure. Much of the old Scotch-Irish folk lore and many of the old country superstitions, weeded out elsewhere by modern education and public opinion, are still alive and flourishing in the mountains, much added to

Kentucky (continued)

and embellished upon by the well known Irish wit, at it's best in these hills.

Another reason for this superstition, is their poor education and almost total lack of reading material, including newspapers. School keeps but five or six months a year under poorly trained teachers and with no adequate supplies. In my home city, just before the Allocation Board holds its annual meeting to decide how much is to go to the schools, how much to the city government, and how much to the county government, when everyone is madly scrambling to get the lion's share, there is always a great hue and cry about the pathetic state of our schools and their great need of new educational facilities. When I stood in that dirty little one room school house I visited in the mountains and viewed their pitiful supply, comparing it with my modern well-stocked class room in North, the fallacy of that sacred clause, "All men are created equal" was sharply driven home.

The desks in that dingy little room looked a hundred years old. If they had ever seen paint or varnish, there were no signs of it, nor like-wise of soap and water. They were dirty and carved and written on, but none of them, I noticed, bore wads of gum, as is always true in the North. The books were as old as the desks, torn and filthy, full of vulgar drawings and obscene words. There were no maps, reference books, nor any other aids to learning. Still these children were citizens of the same country and would fight for the same flag as those children in the Northern city where I taught. When I remembered the stock of supplies I seldom used, the broadcasting hook-up in our building, the telephones, the spacious library, the movie, the drinking fountains and lavatories, the beautiful pictures and statues, I was overcome by the unfairness of it all.

As a child, I had read of the Moonlight Schools of this district, and, at one time, had seen educational slides to show what our Home Missionary Fund was doing there. All I have to say is that those moonlight rays never shone upon the mountaineer schools I visited, and none of the contributions I had given to that worthy cause ever reached this group I saw.

There are very few radios in the mountains, and many children grow up without ever seeing a movie. It is but natural that they would grasp their only opportunity of hearing a good story by sitting at the knee of some old woman, who, in her own childish credulity, repeats the tales her ancestors told to her, always, of course, with proper improvements, and always, to give her story a realistic touch, casting for its hero or heroine, some local character, or not too distant relative.

Not only do the children listen to the tales, but the grown up men and women as well. Mountaineers seem to have very little else to do. They get up to see the sun rise because they go to bed early, and after the men hoe their little corn or tobacco patch and the women wash the dishes, make the beds, and sweep the rough puncheon floors, they all assemble on the front stoop and listen to "Maw" or some other elderly women spin yarns. I wish my six year old daughter would ever once listen to me with the round eyed trusting attention I saw men of forty give these old crones. Whether it was the credulity of the listener or the mountaineer's unfailing courtesy to the old, they listened and I listened with them. Some of those tales I will repeat.

One of Aunt Het's favorites was a story with a moral. It seemed there was a woman (Aunt Het explained exactly who she was and where she lived, but I won't go into that), who never could get her hair arranged to please her when she went to meetin' on Sunday. She was a very pretty woman, but her temper was rather short. Each moment that she stood before her mirror trying to fix her hair just right, she would grow more and more angry. One day, in exasperation, she stamped her foot and exclaimed she had rather die and go to Hell as to go to church with her hair looking a fright.

A few days later, she fell sick and died. Her funeral was a large one, (Aunt Het was there in person), and was held at the church. Every thing went according to schedule until it was time to start for the cemetery. The four pall-bearers, big strong men, (Aunt Het named them all), started to carry out the casket, but for some reason, they could not move it. Two more men stepped up to help, but they couldn't budge it either, though they lifted with all their might. This seemed strange as the corpse had been a very slender woman. The situation grew tense. Others offered their assistance until twelve of the strongest men in the community were lifting on the casket. It was of no use. The minister called for a hammer and chisel and began to

Kentucky (continued)

pry up the lid. No sooner was that casket opened than a huge black cat jumped out and ran through the door. The poor woman had evidently got her wish and gone straight to Hell.

Another story that always enchanted me was about a reckless young man who was breaking his dear mother's and sister's hearts by the wild life he led. One night, when he was riding home from a drunken brawl, too intoxicated to manage his steed, he was thrown from the saddle and his neck was broken. They had a beautiful funeral for him, (Aunt Het attended that one, too), and a fine tombstone was erected at the head of his grave. No one could comfort his mother and sister, both Christian women, because he had died a sinner and they were afraid his soul was damned. Each day they would go and water his grave with their tears and pray for him. One morning when they neared the place, they noticed an engraved inscription raised on the stone. Approaching they read,

"Between the stirrup and the ground, Mercy was
sought and mercy was found."

Aunt Het was always going to take me to that cemetery and show me that very stone, but somehow she never got round to it.

There were many "hanted" places in Kentucky, one where Aunt Het had lived, The Meadows, which had been one of the bloody battle grounds of the Civil War. No one could ever sleep in that house, because as soon as night came, the moans and curses of the ghosts of the dead soldiers would begin. They would even go so far as to chase each other around the house. Aunt Het once saw a headless one, wielding a sword, and it nearly frightened her out of her wits. It was a fine house, but she made my uncle move from there.

There are certain roads in Kentucky, where murders have been committed that no one ever dares travel on at night. All mountaineers, no matter how brave, steer clear of those places. Those who do not, always come to some bad end.

Dreams are most important in the mountains. They are always related in detail and listened to with respect. Just about everybody, too, seems to dream. Perhaps, after all, it is an enchanted region. Maybe the reason for its people remaining the same is because a spell has been cast over those hills and they are unable to change. If so, I

Kentucky (continued)

hope that spell will not be entirely broken until the war is over and I can visit there again. Illiterate the mountaineers may be, but they are altogether hospitable, entertaining, and kind, and I'm not sure but what they have discovered the secret of a contented existence. Encircled and folded in by their mountains and hazy, blue skies, they have time to rest and talk and think. In a busy life like ours who could wish for more?

The End

About Mother

I was the ninth child in a family of twelve. My father had been a teacher as a young man in Kentucky, but had moved to a farm in northern Michigan before I was born. Life was never dull in our home. Everyone liked to talk, or discuss heatedly any and all subjects. My father took part in and encouraged these debates, usually based on historical or political questions, but anything would serve. I learned the finer points of rebuttal in a hard school. I never got to say much myself, and I hated the noise when Father and two or three brothers got started. I spent most of my time reading. I attended a country school that, though poorly equipped in most ways, had a fine library of classic literature. Being subject to colds as well as shy, I was allowed to stay in and read my recesses. I finished the eighth grade as valedictorian, with a good literary background, but bashful and awkward and scared to death of people. My sister, who was two years older, but in the same grade, and I boarded in town with an old lady while we attended high school. My father had chosen her because she would see that we did not go out with boys. I had little social training in high school, but made a good scholastic record, graduating as valedictorian. My sister and I went to normal college determined to get a life certificate. Here I entered literary and debating clubs, and received some attention for original poetry and stories. We worked our way through school, however, and had little time for social life.

So, at the age of 19, I became a teacher in high school, shy with many opinions, but afraid to express them. Naturally, I was forced to assume leadership. Children liked me, even fellow teachers liked to hear me talk, and began to call upon me more and more to take responsibility. Two years later I went to Flint to teach. There I taught in the same junior high school for twenty years. During that time I married and raised two daughters, but kept on with my work. I took a more active part in public life. I did much church work, and became much interested in helping young people. People liked me. My opinions were respected. I am afraid I got pretty sure of myself. Then because of health, I moved to northern Michigan to a small town. I found that my opinions were neither valued or desired. At first I was hurt, than amused. Now, after six years, I am happy to feel I am becoming integrated. I hope I've lived down my first impression. But I'm still not so sure that I offer any advice unsolicited, even though it's hard to keep still.

Lelia

135

To order additional copies of **The Plan, Collected Short Stories & Poems of Mary Lelia Allen Smith,** complete the following:

Ship to: *(please print)*

Name _____

Address_____

City/State/Zip_____

_____ copy(ies) of **The Plan** @ $12.00 each $_____

Postage and handling @ $2.00 per book $_____

Michigan residents add 6% sales tax $_____

Total amount enclosed $_____

Gift Card Message:_____

From: _____

Make checks payable to: **A.R.D. Service, Inc.**

Send to: **A.R.D. Service, Inc.**
1250 Rankin • Unit F • Troy, MI 48083 • (810) 585-2900

- -

To order additional copies of **The Plan, Collected Short Stories & Poems of Mary Lelia Allen Smith,** complete the following:

Ship to: *(please print)*

Name _____

Address_____

City/State/Zip_____

_____ copy(ies) of **The Plan** @ $12.00 each $_____

Postage and handling @ $2.00 per book $_____

Michigan residents add 6% sales tax $_____

Total amount enclosed $_____

Gift Card Message:_____

From: _____

Make checks payable to: **A.R.D. Service, Inc.**

Send to: **A.R.D. Service, Inc.**
1250 Rankin • Unit F • Troy, MI 48083 • (810) 585-2900